ANCIENT LANGUAGES OF THE HISPANIC PENINSULA

James M. Anderson

UNIVERSITY
PRESS OF
AMERICA

Lanham • New York • London

Copyright © 1988 by

University Press of America,® Inc.

4720 Boston Way
Lanham, MD 20706

3 Henrietta Street
London WC2E 8LU England

Printed in the United States of America

British Cataloging in Publication Information Available

Library of Congress Cataloging-in-Publication Data

Anderson, James Maxwell, 1933-
Ancient languages of the Hispanic peninsula.

Bibliography: p.
1. Spain—Languages.   2. Portugal—Languages.
3. Inscriptions, Iberian.   4. Inscriptions, Celtiberian.
5. Inscriptions, Ancient—Portugal.   I. Title.
P1081.A53 1988   409'.366   87-29575
ISBN 0-8191-6731-2 (alk. paper)
ISBN 0-8191-6732-0 (pbk. : alk. paper)

All University Press of America books are produced on acid-free
paper which exceeds the minimum standards set by the National
Historical Publications and Records Commission.

For Jürgen and Bertha

TABLE OF CONTENTS

LIST OF FIGURES

Figure		Page

LIST OF MAPS

PREFACE

The history of Spain and Portugal, for most students, begins with the Roman conquest of the peninsula. The period preceding, however, while still often vague in specifics, emerges out of the linguistic and archaeological record as a time of sweeping change and of no small importance to the early history of Mediterranean affairs.

Amalgamation of external cultural features brought the inhabitants of the Iberian peninsula out of the Stone Age and some Hispanic peoples rose to meet the challenges of contemporary civilization emanating from the east, as attested by the adoption of a writing system of eastern Mediterranean provenance.

In the first millennium B.C., Phoenicians, Greeks and Celts entered the peninsula, the first two spawning a written legacy, the latter an ethnic and cultural presence that persists to this day. Many of the innovative features, however, were later swept away by the rising tide of Roman conquest.

Our perception of this period leans heavily on archaeology and to a lesser extent on the testimony of ancient authors who were often contemporary or near contemporary with the material evidence. Of the various kinds of durable material such as pottery, stone sculptures and jewelry, the potentially most valuable artifacts are the native texts which speak directly to us about the events of the time. These inscriptions, while still in large part undeciphered and thus depriving us of much of their significance, are, nevertheless, of paramount interest in piecing together the geographical distribution and cultural affinities of the various Hispanic peoples.

From a linguistic point of view, this ancient documentation reveals the diversity of language on the peninsula, relationships with known languages within and beyond the Pyrenean frontier, and cultural contacts that resulted in lexical borrowings. Some of the texts help classify the languages and in conjunction with place names, present insight into migration routes and population movements. They help delimit the distribution of peoples and cultures and they tell us something about the structure and patterns of the languages in question.

The primary theme of this book centers on the ancient texts, most of whose underlying languages are now extinct but partially recoverable from the documentation.

The purpose of this introductory text is to bring to the reader an awareness of the Hispanic civilizations in these remote times and to present an overview of their languages and inscriptions, aspects of their cultural affinities and physical manifestations. It is not the intention to pursue controversial subjects relating to this early history, but rather to present as nearly as possible an orientation in which most accounts agree.

J.M.A.

Calgary, 1987

ACKNOWLEDGMENTS

Financial support for the research underlying this monograph was generously given by the Canada Council, by the Social Sciences and Humanities Research Council of Canada and by the University of Calgary. Further valuable assistance was given by Dr. Jaime Siles in supplying documentation of often difficult access, by Fletcher Valls, then curator of the Archeological Museum of Valencia who without hesitation allowed full use of all the resources at his disposal including his own sometimes unpublished work on Iberian inscriptions, by the late Professors Antonio Tovar and Ulrich Schmoll whose suggestions and guidance were of considerable assistance and by Professor Jürgen Untermann of the University of Cologne who always found time in a busy schedule to lend his expertise, his extensive library, and indeed even his house as a research center for the production of this book. No small part of this munificence I owe to Mrs. Bertha Untermann and it is with great pleasure that I dedicate this book to them.

For clerical assistance, I would like to thank Kathy Officer, Lynda Costello and Renate Hull; for artwork, Linda LeGeyt.; for technical assistance, Sandy Buker, Pavel Kubicek and Dr. Rodney Roche. A final acknowledgment goes to Sherry Anderson for many laborious hours of typing, sorting and keeping records and to Siwan and Corri, introduced to the world of ancient inscriptions before they could read.

Chapter 1

INTRODUCTION

Throughout the million or so years that the Hispanic peninsula has been inhabited, numerous cultures have come and disappeared, some identified only by vestigal traces of human remains, others by monumental structures of enduring stone. From early primitive tools and weapons to megalithic burial tombs and fortified towns, the kaleidoscopic array of cultural changes of paleolithic to modern times is gradually being put into perspective. The influences that shaped the Hispanic scene appear to have been primarily of European and East Mediterranean provenance, although North Africa also played a part which reached its climax in a later day when the peninsula was absorbed into the Arabic world.

The introduction of bronze metallurgy into the Hispanic peninsula about 3000 B.C., substantially altered the social make-up of the Neolithic settlements and transformed the peninsular demography as the rise of urban life attracted people from the country, and social classes developed, presumably on the basis of relative skills in the new industries. Regions endowed with abundant metal deposits became centres of attraction, especially the valley of the Guadalquivir, Almería, Granada, certain areas of Portugal, and the northwest, where deposits of tin were plentiful.

Fig. 1.   Megalithic Tomb Drawing

Associated with the initial phases of the Bronze Age in Spain are Aegean artifacts, fortified villages and collective burial sites such as those of Los Millares near Almería and Vila Nova de Sãn Pedro in central Portugal. The later El Argar site, also near Almería (1800-1000 B.C.) appears also to have been in trading contact with the east, and may owe its origins to immigration from western Greece.

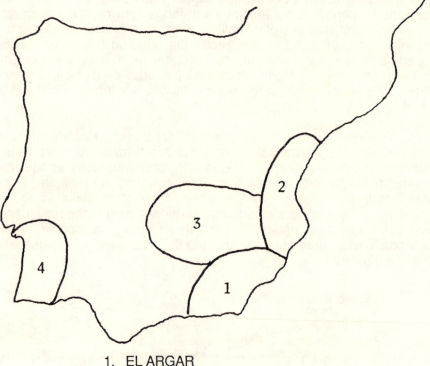

1. EL ARGAR
2. VALENCIAN
3. LA MANCHA
4. SOUTHERN PORTUGAL

Map 1.   Hispanic Bronze Age Cultures Based on Tuñón de Lara, p. 87

Near the end of the Bronze Age, however (about 800 B.C.), occurred the first clear and substantial contacts of the Hispanic inhabitants with eastern Mediterranean Phoenicians, and a little later with Greek sailors and merchants. About the same period, the first Indo-European peoples crossed the Pyrenees into Spain.

These newcomers to the Hispanic peninsula encountered societies already established along the Mediterranean seaboard, whose similarities in language, art and architecture suggest a loose conglomerate of independent communities. These people, the Iberians, of unknown origins, who may have been simply a continuation of Neolithic or early Bronze Age cultures, appear to have deflected the trans-Pyrenean Indo-European speakers away from the fertile coastal areas onto less desirable and sparsely inhabited regions of the meseta.

The southwest corner of the peninsula (Southern Portugal and Western Andalucía), meanwhile, was inhabited by the so-called Tartessians, a designation based on the semi-mythical kingdom of Tartessos located in this part of the world by the Greeks. Also of unknown origins the Tartessians appear to have been unrelated to the Iberians.

In the northeast quadrant of Spain dwelt the ancestors of the Basques--again a people of undetermined provenance whose language, the only survivor of the ancient Iberian vernaculars, appears unique, an isolate, among the world's tongues.

In general, the Phoenicians were occupied with the southern coastal regions of the peninsula, including the Atlantic fringes of Portugal, while the Greeks, eventually inhibited in this area by Punic interests, exploited the northeastern littoral. Along the Mediterranean seaboard, both were in contact with the local autocthonous inhabitants, the Iberians. The Celtic tribes who entered Spain in several migrations through the Pyrenees, fanned out over the meseta and the northwest, ultimately reaching the Atlantic coasts sometime prior to 500 B.C.

The Roman historian, Velleius, of the time of the Emperor Tiberius, places the date of the founding of Gadir (modern Cádiz) in 1100 B.C. Modern historians and archaeologists accept or deny the twelfth century starting point of Gadir, according to how much weight they feel justified in attributing to secondary sources which sometimes conflict with archaeological evidence.

Archaeological data suggest Phoenician sites and navigation routes to Spain had not begun before the ninth century, B.C.[1] Other sites inside the Straits of Gibraltar along the Spanish coast, such as Málaga and Almuñecar (Sexi), appear to have been established in the eighth or seventh century, B.C., and contain Phoenician, Greek and Cypriot artifacts from this period. In the past several decades discoveries along the south coast of Spain, especially east of Málaga, have brought to light several small Phoenician sites. Near the mouth of the river Vélez, for example, five small *factorías* existed in only four square kilometers. They appear to have been established in the eighth century B.C., reached maximum production in the seventh, declined in the sixth, and subsequently were abandoned.

Phoenician and Punic incursions into Spain and Portugal along the Mediterranean and Atlantic coastal fringes have left traces of their passage in a few place names. Oftentimes, however, these names were obliterated by Latin and Arabic influences of a later time. The name Cádiz from Gadir 'fortress' cf. Arabic *gadis*, a name also found in the southern Moroccan town of Agadir, was of Phoenician origin, as well as the names of Málaga (from Malaca), Cartagena, Ibiza and Mahón. The ancient name of Fuengirola was Suel.

The reputed earliest contacts of the Greeks with inhabitants of the western Mediterranean in the second millennium, B.C. are obscure and interspersed with legend and mythology. Vague references also allude to sailors from Rhodes who visited the Balearic Islands and founded the town of Rhode on the mainland Spanish coast, a little south of the Pyrenean mountains. Seamen from Samos are purported to have discovered the rich markets of southern Spain and Tartessos through the voyage of Kolaios (according to Herodotos) about 620-630 B.C.[2]

About 600 B.C., the Phocaeans founded Massalia (Marseilles) and from this commanding position on the northern arc of the Mediterranean they expanded westward and established colonies along the Spanish coasts. The founding of Emporion occurred a little before 550 B.C. and this came to constitute the most important Greek settlement on the peninsula down to Roman times. Situated on the Bay of Rosas in sight of the lofty peaks of the Pyrenees, the city flourished behind its stout walls which enclosed about 26,000 square meters and contained a market, temples, the *agora*, streets and houses and all the usual features of a Greek city. Both Emporion and Rhode close by which appears to have been resettled, minted their own money and carried on a lively commerce. Greek urban development in Catalonia was a continuation of their commercial activity in Provence and Languedoc.

This expansion continued along the Catalan, Valencian, Murcian and Andalucían coasts documented, albeit rather imprecisely, by classical authors who refer to Greek implantations along the Valencian littoral such as *Hemeroscopeion, Alonis* and *Akra Leuke* and *Mainake* in Andalucía in the vicinity of Málaga. Ancient tradition considered these places to have been cities of some importance but their presence has not yet been confirmed by archaeological discoveries. Mainake, in fact, was situated in an area where only Phoenician sites have been identified from about the same period.

It would seem that the Valencian sites were not as important as ancient authors suggested and while small colonies probably existed in these areas, they did not reach a status comparable to Emporion.

Greek exploration and establishment of colonies on the Hispanic peninsula seems to have followed chronologically that of the

4

Phoenicians as there is little to demonstrate significant Greek contacts in Spain before the seventh century, B.C. The Phoenicians dominated certain tracts of the southern coasts while the primary impact of Greek civilization was felt in the north--in Catalonia and less so along the eastern and southeastern coastal areas.

Other Phocaean colonies or trading stations were thought to have been established near the mouth of the river Ebro such as Hyops and Lebendontia along with Kypsela and Pyrene near the Cabo de Creus, Kallipolis near Tarragona and a few others.[3]

The majority of Greek place names, plentiful in antiquity, have disappeared. Rosas is one of the exceptions and is derived from Rhodes, and Ampurias is related to *emporion* 'market place.' Other Greek names were replaced by Latin and Arabic and still others were simply abandoned along with the site, for example Kallipolis is no longer, Acra Leuke 'white rock' is perhaps now Alicante, and the island of pines, Pituoussa, gave way to the Punic name, Ibiza. Greek presence in Spain, and contact with the Iberians is aptly demonstrated by several important inscriptions.

Written in an Ionic Greek alphabet of about the sixth century, B.C., but corresponding to the local language, the Alcoy Lead Tablet, found at what appears to have been an Iberian sanctuary on the summit of a

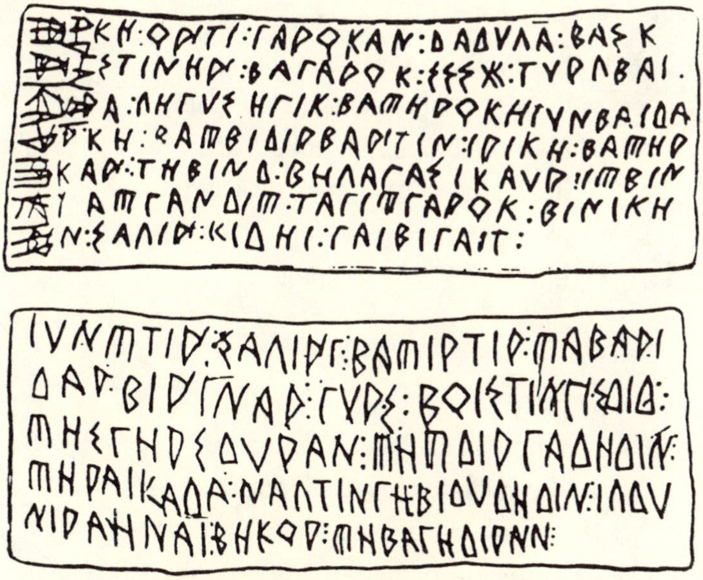

Fig. 2a The Alcoy Lead Tablet
After Gómez-Moreno (1962) pp. 69-70

mountain in the vicinity of Alcoy (near Alicante), is a rectangular lead plaque incised on both sides.[4] Another, the Cigarralejo Lead,[5] was discovered in a necropolis of that name in the vicinity of Mula. The same writing system was employed for both inscriptions which are in the same language.

On the Alcoy tablet, the lines of writing are straight and parallel and the writing can be characterized as stoichedon, although far from perfect. The Cigarrelejo document, on the other hand, displays a form of writing running in curves and approaching boustrophedon style, or perhaps, more appropriately, *Schlangenschrift*. Words were separated by vertical dots in the manner of other Mediterranean inscriptions including early Greek, and the direction of writing was from left to right.

Inscribed in the left hand margin of the plaque from top to bottom and apparently superimposed on the principle text are the words:

ar'nai şakarişker

The remainder of the inscription is clear and offers little difficulty in transliteration.

Side I

irike or'ti garokan dadula bask

buistiner' bagarok sss? turlbai

lura legusegik başerokeiunbaida

urke başbidirbar'tin irike başer

okar' tebind belagasikaur işbin

ai aşgandiş tagişgarok binike

bin salir' kidei gaibigait

Side II

iunştir salir'g başirtir şabari

dar bir'inar gurs boistingisdid

şesgersduran şeşdirgadedin

şeraikala naltinge bidudedin ildu

niraenai bekor şebagediran

Fig. 2b   Transliteration of the Alcoy Lead Tablet

6

The lead tablet from the necropolis of Cigarrelejo at Mula, thirty kilometers from Murcia, was found in a grave with other artifacts which were datable to the third century, B.C.[6] The tablet, lacking elegance and partially obliterated, is reminiscent in the direction of writing of some of the inscriptions from southern Portugal. Note, also, the exiguous use of vertical dots as word separation markers.

Fig. 3a   The Cigarralejo Lead Tablet
After Gómez-Moreno (1962)

iuntegen ş . . .
şakarbik şoş . . .
lagutas kebeş . . .
işgenuş andinue . biandingor'şanlenebar'er'beigulnarer'ganikboş
tarikedelbabineditarke . . .nela ebanalbaşuşbeliginela
sabarbaşderikbidedenedişbeşanelaş
ikbaideşuişebar'tasartiduragunan

Fig. 3b   Transliteration of the Cigarralejo Lead Tablet

7

From the small island of Illeta, a little north of Alicante, come another pair of short incomplete inscriptions on ceramic material in Greek lettering and relating to a site occupied since Neolithic times, but which flourished moderately between the fourth and third centuries, B.C.[7]

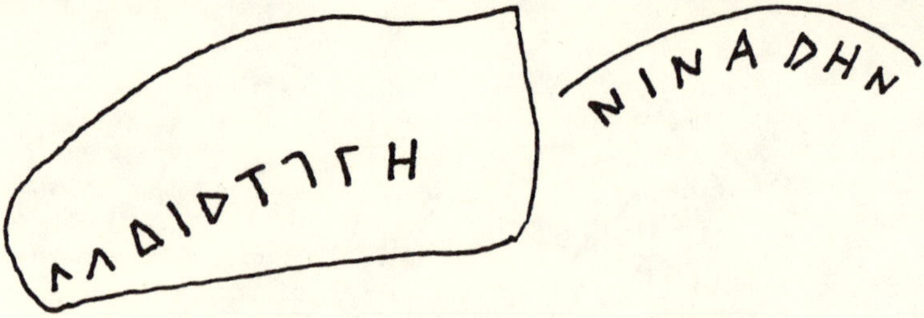

ildirtige ninaren

Fig 4. The Illeta Inscriptions and Transliteration after J. Untermann to appear in Monumentum Linguarum Hispanicarum Vol. 3

The Alcoy and Cigarrelejo lead tablets display several modifications from the Greek alphabet employed about the sixth century B.C. Some of the Greek signs were not utilized at all, suggesting the lack of equivalent sounds in the Iberian language spoken around Alcoy and Mula. It is not clear, of course, that all the signs inscribed on the tablets had the same phonetic values as they had in Greek, nor that all the sounds in the language were represented in the inscriptions. Other modifications revolved around the angular form of the *O*, i.e., ◊; two types of *r* signs, i.e., I> [*r*] and I>' [*r'*]that appear to represent two distinct sounds, and two signs for sibilant sounds ξ and ϻ transcribed here as [*s*] and [*ṣ*], respectively.

A comparison of words, or at least phonological sequences, helps to isolate what appear to be morpheme boundaries not otherwise delimited by a vertical series of dots.

Alcoy	**Cigarralejo**
un-baida	ik-baida
-rike	ta-rike
iun-ṣtir'	iun-tegen
ṣabar-idar	ṣabar-baṣ
ṣakar-iṣker	ṣakar-bes
aṣ-gan-di-ṣ	gan-ik-bos
bar't-in	bar't-as
bi-du-dedin	bi-deden-e

While the inscriptions in the Greek alphabet are few in number, they offer a glimpse into the structure of the Iberian language underlying them.

Similarities in vocabulary between the Alcoy and Cigarralejo tablets and inscriptions in the semi-syllabic Hispanic writing discussed in chapter 2, suggest related languages or dialects throughout the Iberian zone, cf.

Alcoy	Cigarriejo	Other Inscriptions	
bai	bai	bai	(Ullastret)
baida	baide	baide	(Castellón)
-dira-		adir	(Liria)
-edin	andin	adin	(Ascoli Bronze)
	eban-	eban	(Sagunto, Liria)
	-ebari	eberi	(Fraga, abari)
	eŕibe	erebai	(Liria)
ildunir (Illeta *ildir*)		ildir	(Liria)
iunstir'		iumstir̯	(Bechi)
gai		gai	(Liria)
gandiṣ	gani-	ganides	(Liria)
ṣakariṣker	sakarbeṣ	sakarisker̯	(Liria)
		sakarbiṣka	(Mogente)
	-ṣuiṣe-	-suise-	(Ascoli Bronze)
-urke		ur̯ke	(Castellón)

In spite of the deficiency of signs in the Hispanic epichoric scripts (discussed later) to distinguish voiceless (tense) and voiced (lax) occlusives, such contrasts, seem to have occurred in the Greek alphabet texts, cf.

	T	K			T	K
Ʒ	Δ	Γ	=	b	d	g

The alphabet employed in the Greek script documents consisted of the following:

Λ	a	H	e	N	n	⟨	s
Ʒ	b	I	i	◊	o	⋔	ṣ
Γ	g	K	k	I>	r	T	t
Δ	d	Λ	l	I>	r'	V	u

Conspicuous for its absence is the sign Π for [p] indicating the lack of a voiceless-voiced labial contrast.

The phonological paradigm based on the signs in the Greek script inscriptions can be presented as:

Consonants			Vowels	
-	t	k	i	u
b	d	g	e	o
	s	ş		a
	n			
	l			
	r	r̓		

It should be emphasized here that the apparent opposition between voiceless and voiced contrasts among occlusive consonants is assumed, not proven, since minimal pairs of the type found in, say, English *pit/bit, ten/den*, etc., which reflect a difference in meaning, are not available in the Iberian texts. Some analogous examples of possible contrasts must suffice, for instance,

şakar-	başirtir
bagar-	başbidir

The use of a Greek alphabet in writing the Iberian language demonstrates that lexical forms may sometimes terminate in an occlusive consonant, a fact obscured by the Iberian syllabic signs for these sounds. Compare the following from the Alcoy Lead Tablet:

gaibigait	-t
tebind	-d
bagarok	-k
salir̓g	-g

Similarly, the alphabetic script indicates that certain combinations of sounds are rare or non-existent. Combinations of occlusives such as *bt, gd, tk,* (with the possible exception of *kb* as in *ikbaida*) do not occur, nor do sequences of the type occlusive plus non-occlusive consonants such as *ts, dn, kl,gr.*

The place and manner of articulation of the two types of sibilant sounds, namely, ⊓ and ⟨ , is not clear; nor is that of the two liquid type sounds represented by ⟨⟩ and ⟨⟩ .

A major problem in Iberian studies is the difficulty in penetrating the morphological structure even within purely distributional parameters, a matter which precludes a broader comprehension of the syntax. Are *-ri* and *-ir* the same ending, e.g. *șabari, iunștir,* reordered along the lines of *-ri* to *-ir* in avoidance of sequences such as *tr* (**iunștri*) a non-permissible sequence in the language?

Without knowledge of the meaning, we cannot know if *ri* and *ir* are reordered sequences of the same morpheme, independent units, or simply orthographic sequences devoid of semantic content.

Another much later document, this time employing the Roman alphabet to record Iberian/Basque personal and place names, is also of paramount importance for Iberian studies. Discovered in Rome in 1908 and preserved in the Palazzo dei Conservatori, the Ascoli Bronze plaque, also known as the *Turma Salluitana,* is one of the most important documents extant pertaining to ancient Iberian studies. The inscription contains the names of thirty Iberian horse soldiers whose troop (Turma) distinguished itself in battle during a campaign in Asculum in 89 B.C., the social or Marsic War, for which the soldiers earned the honor of Roman citizenship and their names immortalized in bronze:

The names formed a troop   from the region of the major city of Salluia (Salluitana) - on Iberian coins Salduie - called Caesaraugusta during Roman Imperial times, today Zaragoza.

Individuals are recorded in accordance with more precise locations under geographical headings such as Ilerdenses (for Lérida) but not all sites have been identified.

Damage to the plaque has obliterated some of the names, but the remainder have been useful in clarifying some aspects of the linguistic structure of the ancient Iberian language. The names inscribed on the plaque are, in each case, followed by the letter *f* to designate *filius* 'son of' added by the Roman scribe. The second name, then, is that of the father.

Similarities between Basque names and those inscribed on the Ascoli plaque leave little doubt as to a certain commonalty.

sanibelser adingibas f
illurtibas bilustibas f
estopeles ordennas f
torsinno austinco f
bagarensis
cacususin chadar f
  . . ucenses
  . . . sosimilus f
  . . . irsecel f
  . . . elgaun f
  . . nespaiser f
    ilerdenses
c otacilius suisetarten f
cn cornelius nesille f
p eabius enasagin f
    becensis
turtumelis atanscer f
    segienses
sosinaden sosinasae f
sosimilus sosinasae f
urgidar luspanar f
gurtarno biurno f
elandus enneges f
agirnes bennabels f

nalbeaden agerdo f
arranes arbiscar f
umargibas luspangib f
    ennecensis
beles umarbeles f
turinnus adimels f
ordumeles burdo f
    libenses
bastugitas adimels f
umarillum tarbantu f
    succonsenses
belennes albennes f
atullo tautindals f
illuersenses
balciadin balcibil f

Fig. 5 Names Inscribed on the Ascoli Bronze Tablet

Ascoli	Basque
agirnes	aquirre
albennes	albéniz
enneges	enneco
estopeles	estibaliz
arranes	arana
gurtarno	gortazar
bilustibas	berástegui
illurtibas	illurdo
ordumeles	ordoño
turinnus	turina

In addition, parts of several appelatives occur in both:[2]

Ascoli	Basque	
sosin-	zuzen	'right, fair'
umar-	ume	'litter'
biur-	bi(h)ur	'twisted'
beles, bels	beltz	'black' (cf. also <u>bele</u> 'raven')
-iskar	ezker	'left handed'
arranes	arren	'lame'
umari<u>llum</u>	il(h)un	'dark'

The obvious parallel between the Ascoli plaque and certain names in Basque has suggested to some scholars that the *Turma Salluitana* was a Basque contingent in the Roman army, but turning our attention to Iberian inscriptions, we find also much in common with this inscription in both proper names and linguistic structural features.

An Iberian gravestone inscription from Iglesuela del Cid reads in transliteration *ildubeleşeban* where the sequences *ildu* (Ascoli Bronze *illu-*) and *beleş* clearly conform to the names of the *Turma Salluitana*. Compare also several inscriptional forms from Sagunto: *balkeadin* and *ikorbeles*; from Azaila *ilduradin*; from Castellón *biuṛu*, *sosin-* and *uṛge-*.

Among the names on the Ascoli Bronze the second name or some part of it is often repeated in the first name, cf.

umar<u>gib</u>as	luspan<u>gib</u>
<u>beles</u>	umar<u>beles</u>
illur<u>tibas</u>	bilus<u>tibas</u>
<u>sosin</u>adin	<u>sosin</u>asae
<u>balci</u>adin	<u>balci</u>bil

In several cases, the relationship is somewhat obscure and may reflect a restructuring of phonological or morphological elements:

<u>ordu</u>meles	<u>burdo</u>
<u>gur</u>tar<u>no</u>	bi<u>urno</u>
<u>atu</u>llo	<u>tau</u>tindals
<u>bele</u>n<u>nes</u>	al<u>bennes</u>

While the relationship between the first and second names is not altogether obvious, examples that seem to show no derivational relationships becomes clearer when internal methods of reconstruction are applied.

The general formation of the names in the Ascoli Bronze suggests that some modifications were made with the juxtaposition of certain phonological sequences:

*nb > m (via *mb *mm)

*nd > nn

*ld > ll

adin occurs in *adingibas* and *bels*, *beles* occurs in *bennabels* and *umarbeles*. The name *adimels* appears to consist of these two components, that is, *adin* plus *bels* (or *beles*). The name *umarbeles* would then consist of *unbar-beles*.

Similarly, the name *umarillun* can be reconstructed as *unbar-ildun* and partial confirmation of the reconstructed name comes from other Iberian sources as for example the inscription from Sagunto which reads *nereildun* (*nere-ildun*) and from Azaila where an inscription reads *ilduradin* (*ildu-r-adin*).

One name shows a slightly divergent form from its expected representation. The second element in *esto-peles* is undoubtedly *-beles*, perhaps misrepresented through scribal error. The names *luspanar*, . . . *nespaiser* and others suggest that, after voiceless *s* the voiceless variant of *b* occurred in Iberian but the Iberian syllabary did not record this phonetic characteristic. The Latin alphabet, on the other hand, was well suited to this task.

Underlying forms hint at restructuring rules that require more data to substatiate or repudiate. The name *umarillum tarbantu*, for example, is reconstructed as *unbar-ildun tarbantu*. The name *umargibas luspangib* is fashioned as *unbar-gibas lusban-gib*:

unbar-ildun tarbantu

unbar-gibas lusban-gib

These forms, and a few others displaying similar characteristics, suggest a metathesis rule *ban > nba/___r*. If *ban* can be taken as the base form to which phonological processes are applied, the rule, through the stages *ban + r > *bnar > nbar*, voids the sequence *-nr* and other noncompatible sequences arising from the first change, that is, *bn*.[9]

14

A comparison of some of the foregoing names in a paradigmatic relationship suggests common basic elements such as in the following examples with altered forms of *beles* and *aden* (some forms reconstructed):

*be			nd	a-	(bennabels)
	e	1	and	us	
*be		1	end	es	(belennes)
*al	be		nd	es	(albennes)
nal	be		aden		

The process of name derivation, obscure but discernible in the Ascoli Bronze, also seems to occur in Iberian inscriptions from earlier periods. The similarity in derivation can help to tentatively identify certain sequences of signs as names. An inscription from Azaila reads:

borotenbotenin

The sequence seems to be a name in which the first name utilizes elements of the second name.[10] Similarly, on a wine amphora from Azaila is found the word *bakuborbakora* that suggests a personal name *bakubor bakora*.

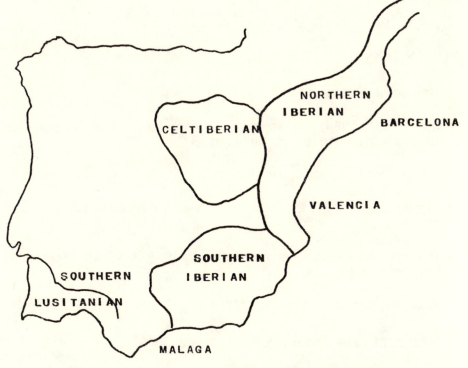

Map 2. Areas of Indigenous Writing Systems

Besides documentation recorded in Greek and Roman alphabetic scripts relating to the Iberian language, the Iberians themselves left their own style of writing. Their partly alphabetic and partly syllabic orthographic system was also employed by Celtiberian populations of the Hispanic peninsula. Further Hispanic zones of indigenous writing can be delineated in terms of North and South Iberian and southern Lusitanian or Tartessian scripts.

The northern script employed by the Iberians covered the most extensive territory extending from southern France to Alicante along the Mediterranean coasts and inland along the Ebro River Valley. The majority of the Southern or Andalucían documents have come from the eastern section of the region, extending roughly from Abenjibre and the River Júcar westward to Porcuna or the ancient capital of Obulco in the province of Jaén.

Similarities between the signs and values strongly suggest that the writing systems employed in both areas were from the same source, unspecified in detail but of eastern Mediterranean models.

FOOTNOTES

[1] See Bosch-Gimpera 1944, p. 167.

[2] Koch, M. 1984, places the first contacts of the Greeks with Tartessus in the 8th and 7th centuries, B.C.

[3] See, for example, Maluquer 1970, p. 92.

[4] Discovered in 1921, the Alcoy Lead Tablet measures 171 x 62 x 1 mm.

[5] The Cigarralejo document, discovered in 1948, is 12 cm. in diameter and 1 mm. in thickness.

[6] According to Gómez-Moreno 1962, p. 67.

[7] *Ibid.*, p. 71. See also Enrique A. Llobregat 1962.

[8] See Michelena 1961 and Gorrochatequi.

9 The relationship between the names on the Ascoli Bronze was first taken up by Schuchardt in 1909.

10 Discovered and published in 1944 by Cabré the form *boroten* was interpreted as the name *Protemus*. Note that [r̥] is read as [ku] by Untermann.

Chapter 2

ANCIENT IBERIAN WRITING

Of the various Hispanic cultures during the centuries prior to the Roman conquest of the peninsula, the Iberians stand out most clearly in art, architecture, and documentation. They left behind decorated ceramics, walled cities and written records of their language on coins, stone, pottery, and on metal plaques.

Advancements in technology and urban development demanding more sophisticated relationships with the concomitant need to keep accounts of commodities, property, legal pronouncements and obsequies may have contributed to a certain urgency among the ancient Iberians for permanent records. These exigencies were met by developing a local set of signs through borrowing and innovation that came to constitute a system of writing.

The model for writing, perhaps initially in the form of potters' marks, was clearly introduced from the outside, but when and where and by whom still constitutes an enigma.

The largest number of ancient Hispanic inscriptions has come from the coastal areas extending from Andalucía to southern France with the greatest concentration in the region around Valencia. Iberian territory and influence also spread westward into the Celtic settlements of the middle and upper Ebro river valley where their writing was employed by the Celts to record their own Indo-European language. Iberian inscriptions have been unearthed in sufficient numbers and in such humble dwellings as to suggest the use of writing among most classes of society.

From a present perspective, writing on the Hispanic peninsula appeared suddenly and dramatically. It was not, as was often the case elsewhere, preceded by evolutionary manifestations of graphic symbolism such as pictographs, word writing or hieroglyphics, but emerged precipitously as a sophisticated system of arbitrary signs sometime between the years 450-550 B.C.[1]

The antecedents of the ancient Hispanic orthography apparently introduced onto the peninsula would have been concurrent with the infusion of other cultural features relating to style and technique in architecture, armaments, sculpture, ceramics and jewelry, primarily of Greek origin.

To a large degree, foreign influences stemmed from the attraction the peninsula offered in terms of a relatively unexploited country rich in

19

metals (gold, silver, tin, copper) whose enticements led to settlements along the Mediterranean and Atlantic littoral.

Among Iberian systems of writing, about 70% of the signs have counterparts which appeared earlier in Greece. Major Greek contact with the Hispanic peninsula occurred at the end of the fifth century, B.C. During the fourth century, Hellenic influences emanating from Emporion (on the Mediterranean coast a little south of the Pyrenees) were incisive in the realm of ceramics, architecture and sculpture. The Greek model for writing at that time, however, would have been an alphabetic system, yet the Iberian orthography is partly syllabic. The only syllabary employed by the Greeks in the fifth century was in use on Cyprus.

If we assume a monogenetic origin of the Iberian orthography, we must also assume that it was devised under several diverse influences. The Phoenicians, as well as the Greeks, were also on the Hispanic peninsula prior to and during the time Hispanic writing emerged. The former maintained their exclusive sphere of influence in the southern regions of the peninsula, the latter in the Levante and northeast. The Phoenician script, read from right to left, consisted of a kind of abstract syllabary expressing only consonantal signs. Vowels were unspecified and became specific only in context. That is,

$\langle$ [b] $\rangle$ [n] L [l]

$\rangle\langle$ [ban]

$L\langle$ [bāl]

where $\langle$ may stand for [ba] in one case and [bā] in another.

By utilizing syllabic principles along the lines of Phoenician usage, a sign was allowed to stand for a consonant plus (in the case of Iberian) a concrete vowel. For example

$\wedge$ [ka/ga] $\langle$ [ke/ge] $\int$ [ki/gi]

The one-to-one relationship between sign and sound for vowels, liquids, sibilants and nasals, e.g., $\diagup$ = [n] $\lessgtr$ = [s], appears prompted by Greek influence.

It seems likely that Hispanic scribes employed both Phoenician and Greek models in the process of devising their semi-syllabic orthographic system and that the initial phase of their endeavors occurred in an area where both types of scripts were known, where Phoenician and Greek spheres of influence overlapped. This is assumed since both influences are present in the Hispanic writing, as

20

would not be the case if it were developed strictly in one sphere or the other. The most likely region for this development would have been in the Alicante-Valencia region.[2]

As the use of the script spread south and westward, it would have fallen into the sphere of influence of the Phoenicians and taken on more of the characteristics of their writing practices. The southern scripts are written from right to left, in accordance with this usage. To the north where Greek influence was strong, the orthographic signs became Hellenized and were employed from left to right.

Among southern inscriptional remains, sequences of words are often not separated in accordance with Phoenician tradition (as they were in the Greek zone of interest) by two, three and sometimes more dots in vertical alignment. A few of the orthographic signs employed in the south were exclusively Phoenician and are not found outside the region.

The various indigenous Hispanic scripts are of the same type and, presumably, of the same origin. They have features in common that would not be expected to materialize independently in adjacent areas. Many consonant and vowel sounds are represented by the same or similar sign in both regions, for example, occlusives are uniformly written by a sign which also incorporates a following vowel and in other areas, the orthography omits an apparent distinction between voiced and voiceless consonants which had to be supplied by context.

None of the scripts indicate by diacritics or other notations such features as stress, tone, pitch and length.

By the beginnings of the fourth century, B.C., there appears to have been a widely diffused system of writing stretching from Ensérune north of the Pyrenees to southern Spain. The earliest attested writing appeared on Attic pottery at Ullastret datable to the fifth century, B.C. and the most recent inscriptions of Liria date back to the reign of Augustus around the beginning of the first century, A.D., presenting a time span of nearly five centuries during which the Iberian orthography evolved, diversified and diffused throughout much of the peninsula. In the region of Valencia, the oldest written documentation so far corresponds to the fourth century, B.C.

The Iberians may have found good reason to adopt alphabetic signs for the non-occlusive consonants as they regularly occurred in preconsonantal position (e.g., *lt, rt, nt, st*) as well as in word-final position. Individual signs for vowels may have been employed for similar reasons. Vowels often appeared in sequences (e.g., *ai, au*) and they often began the word. This kind of phonological distribution would not lend itself well to a purely syllabic system of writing.

If used in a syllabic fashion, signs such as liquids, laterals and nasals could have obscured or confused meanings to an impermissible extent insomuch as forms like *bana, bane, bani,* could not be readily distinguished from *ban* if a mandatory vowel were added.

Among the inscriptions of the Levante and Catalonia and extending into southern France, the Greek sphere of interest, the system of orthographic signs appeared as follows:

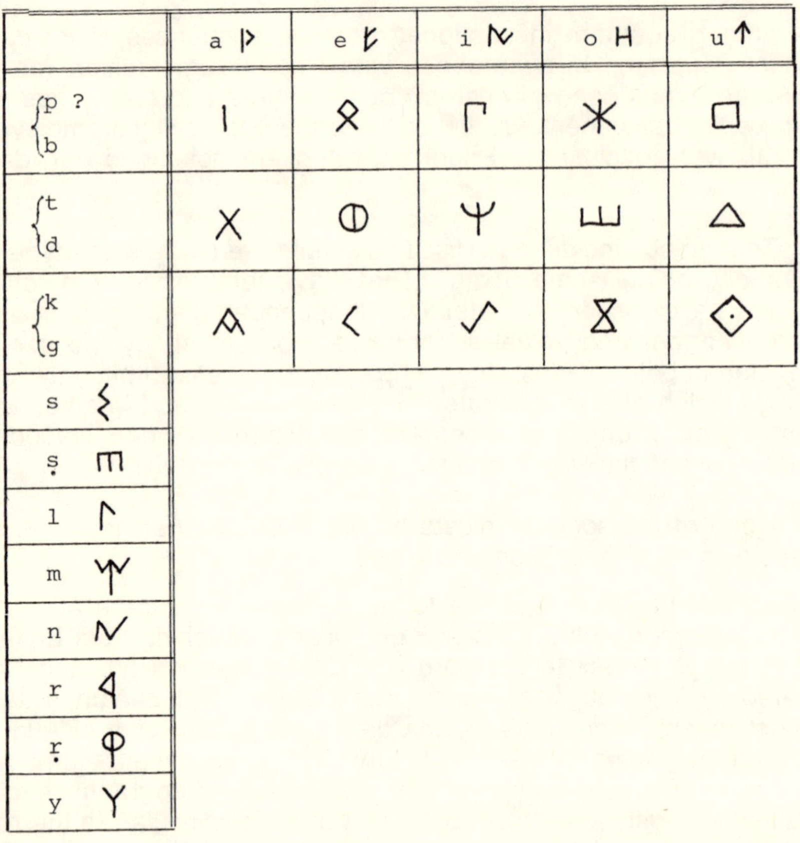

		a ▷	e Ɫ	i ⋔	o H	u ↑
{ p ? \ b		ǀ	⟑	Γ	⁕	▢
{ t \ d		X	⊕	Ψ	⊔	△
{ k \ g		⋀	⟨	⋁	⦸	◇
s	⟨					
ṣ	ⅲ					
l	↑					
m	⋔					
n	Ⅳ					
r	◁					
ṛ	φ					
y	Υ					

Fig. 6.   Iberian Orthographic Signs and Phonetic Equivalents

The sign Υ remains controversial against a background of studies designed to give it its appropriate phonetic place in the system. Resisting a completely satisfactory transliteration, it has generally been associated with a nasal quality primarily due to the fact that it was employed as such in Celtiberian.[3]

A combination of the signs 𝟙𝐫 appears to have given rise to the letter 𝐘 created to depict the sound [m] often the result of an earlier assimilated [-nb-]. The sign and the sound were introduced into the language about the end of the fourth century, B.C. in limited context.[4]

The fact that [p/b, t/d, k/g] were not differentiated in Iberian texts suggests that distinctions could be blurred without undue confusion and that not many words were differentiated on the basis of voiceless/voiced occlusives alone. Presumably, context could be relied upon to distinguish forms and meanings in any ambiguous situation.

The efficiency of a syllabary depends on the internal arrangements of a language. Best suited to this type of writing are languages which allow relatively few syllable types. Japanese is such a language and can be represented orthographically by about fifty syllabic signs. English is not adequately suited with virtually hundreds of syllabic types composed of numerous consonant clusters, e.g., *cv, ccv, ccvc, ccvcc, cccv, cccvccc*, as in *by, spy, spied, spend, stray, strengths.*

In practice, syllabaries were sometimes adapted to languages for which they were badly suited such as the application of the Cypriot syllabary to the Greek language.

A true syllabary, if conceptually consistent, has a separate sign whenever there is a different consonant or vowel within the syllable. In practice, ancient syllabaries did not make all relevant distinctions. A smudging of distinctions among syllables occurred when the use of a single sign represented all syllables sharing the same consonant even though the vowel differed. A system consisting of

ta	da
te	de
ti	di
to	do
tu	du

ideally would have ten signs, but in practice, in Iberian, only five were employed.

Attempts to read the Iberian inscriptions were initiated in the sixteenth century with the enigmatic coin legends generally assumed to have been Greek. Further proclamations on the nature of the Iberian writing and the meanings of the inscriptions were made in the seventeenth and eighteenth centuries, with one school of thought, emanating from Scandinavia, considering the inscriptions to be of Visigothic vintage and written with runic signs, an idea that was never very popular in Spain.

During the course of the eighteenth century, the letters of the Iberian writing system were compared one by one to Greek, Etruscan, Old Latin, Gothic, Phoenician, and Punic, among others, but especially to Greek in the belief that Greek and Phoenician were the languages spoken on the peninsula in preRoman times. Some of these correspondences, of course, still stand today.

Any account of the decipherment of the Hispanic writing systems must include the role played by investigators in the field of numismatics, a discipline which was the single most important factor in unveiling the arcane signs of the ancient Iberians. The process of decoding the Iberian script was achieved through the identification of ancient sites where coins were located by recourse to classical authors and then by a systematic comparison of the coin legend with the classical Greek or Latin name of the site.[5]

For example, ‹ᛕ𐌔𐌔ᛕ and ‹𐌔𐌔ᛕ, legends on Iberian coins, were equated with κισσα referred to by Ptolemy and cissa found in Livy. Similarly, IᛕШΛH seemed to be the same name as βαιτολών (Ptolemy) and ᛕ I▷A the same as ιακκα (Ptolemy).

Non-Latin personal, divine and place names on Latin inscriptions also helped through comparison with names on coin legends to identify the more obscure signs of the Iberian script such as the syllabic signs, as did inscriptions written in a Greek alphabet but in the Iberian language.

The sign I, earlier thought to be a kind of [i]-sound whose articulatory relationship to ᛕ [i] was unclear, was identified as [ba] by Gómez-Moreno from sequences such as I♀ᑕ ᛘ H = [barkino] found on a coin (along with *baitolo* and *basti* on others) and relating to place names in Latin, that is, *Barcino* for Barcelona and Greek *Bastitani*, i.e. the inhabitants of Basti, both mentioned by Pliny in the first century, A.D.

The first Iberian coins were minted before the Roman occupation and reflect an indigenous development but the original model for Iberian coins seems to have been Greek coins and legends which appeared at Emporion inscribed as EMΠOPITΩN 'of the Empurians.'

Three monetary zones stand out on the peninsula: the Levante coastal area and lower Ebro with legends ending in *-sken* and preceded by names of cities or tribes such as *auṣesken* which can be compared with the tribal name *Ausetani*, as attested by Roman historians and geographers; *laieṣken* alongside *Laietani*; *seteiṣken* and *Sedetani*; and *urkesken* comparable to *Urcitani*. The meaning of *-sken* would appear to resemble the Greek coins in meaning, that is, of the *Ausetani* of the *Laietani*, and so on. It could, however, be simply a nominative plural of an ethnic name. These legend types penetrated southward into the eastern part of Andalucía.

The second monetary zone unaffected by Greek models, consisted of Andalucía, but the coin legends in this region adhering to Phoenician models of ancient Gadir (Cádiz), are problematical and little can be stated with surety about their meanings.

The third zone, the region called Celtiberia by the Romans, relates to the mid and upper Ebro valley and interior regions. Here also, are found monetary legends in Iberian script whose names coincide with attested toponyms in classical sources and in the actual toponymy.

Compare:

Lutia	-	lutiakoş
Oncala	-	okalakom
Tierga	-	terkakom

Characterized by the suffix -*ko* the form -*ko-s* is nominative plural in the Celtic language of the area (a suffix that disappeared in Greek and Latin) and -*ko-m* is a genitive plural.

While some mints were in operation before Roman times, their great expansion occurred in conjunction with the progress of the Roman conquest.

*   *   *

One of the most perspicacious numismatic investigators of the nineteenth century was Antonio Delgado whose first volume entitled *Nuevo método de classificación de las medallas autónomas de españa* appeared in 1871. His new transliterations were based on the idea that the Phoenician writing system served as the basis for Hispanic writing and he identified many Iberian signs through comparisons of coin legends with place names recorded by classical authors. These investigations and methods were continued by Zobel de Zangroniz who observed the syllabic value of some of the signs, for example

Λ [ka]   Ⅹ [ko]   △ [du]

These scholars, along with the Belgian, Alois Heiss and his extensive corpus of ancient Hispanic coins, formulated the questions and laid the groundwork for further efforts in Hispanic numismatics.

In his *Monumenta Linguae Ibericae*, published in 1893, Hübner collected all of the Hispanic epigraphic material known up to that time. His conception of the script as entirely alphabetic, however, and consequently erroneous transliterations, attracted few followers to his massive undertaking.

The decade of the 1920's ushered in a new epoch in preRoman Hispanic numismatics and linguistics. Antonio Vives y Escudero in his *La Moneda Hispánica* attempted to group the ancient mints of Spain according to typological-stylistic means. Sources for this undertaking were now greatly expanded. Besides the collected work of others to build upon, he had at his disposal the large and growing coin collections of Madrid and Barcelona, the national Library in Paris and copies of important pieces in the British Museum. Among his assistants, two were of notable scholarly inclination: Pío Beltrán Villagrasa and Gómez-Moreno. The latter decoded the Iberian script in 1922 recognizing, as did Delgado and Zobel, the correctness of the semi-syllabic aspects of the system.

Presented again more definitively in 1943, Gómez-Moreno's views on the subject have now been universally accepted. His system of transliteration incorporated much of the work of earlier investigators as well as his own observations. He thought that the writing system of the Iberians in the northeast of the peninsula proceeded from the older Tartessian script of the south, and that Tartessian writing originated in the eastern Mediterranean.

A few years later, in 1931, G.F. Hill, adhering to the readings of Gómez-Moreno, published his monograph entitled *Notes on the Ancient Coinage of Hispania Citerior* in which he presented a methodology and careful research into chronology and classification that needed only minor corrections by later scholars.

Soon after the end of the Spanish Civil War the *Curso de Numismática* (1942) by Antonio Beltrán Martínez appeared, a book of synthesis which served as handbook for a study of ancient Hispanic coins. It contained a full list of the Iberian coin legends with the transcriptions set out by Gómez-Moreno and information on the location of the ancient mints.

Legends on Hispanic coins ultimately revealed scripts pertaining to Iberian, Celtiberian, southern Lusitanian, Greek, Punic, Libya-Phoenician and Latin languages. The majority of the Iberian and Celtiberian mints belonged to the time between 150 and 70 B.C. but one of the oldest, the silver mint at Sagunto, dates back before the onset of the Roman occupation of the Peninsula in 219 B.C.[6]

Scholarly interest in the Iberian language was not confined to coin legends, however, and in 1942 Pío Beltrán Villagrasa published his monograph *Sobre un interesante vaso escrito de San Miguel de Liria* and again in 1954 one entitled *El plomo escrito de la Bastida (Mogente)*. His was the earliest authoritative work on the Iberian language in a broader context than numismatics. In l946 Julio Caro Barojo published his appraisal of Iberian studies and prepared the groundwork for the geographical distribution of the ancient languages.

Numismatic work continues and has become more precise, more exacting and specific. Fernando Gimeno Rúa studied the Iberian coins with the legend *laieşken* and published his work in 1950, while J.M. de Navascués of the Madrid school of numismatics worked on coins from Sagunto, Calagurris and Celsa. Leandro Villaronga Carriga in 1962 researched the coins with the legend *ikaleşken*.

In 1969, Antonio Manuel de Guadan published his work *Numismática ibérica e ibero-romana* that was, for many years, the standard work on the subject.

Until recently, scholarly interest in Hispanic inscriptions was the domain of archaeologists or ethnographers who had an interest in numismatics and decipherment of ancient texts. The first professional linguist to play a role in Hispanic linguistic antiquities was Antonio Tovar who laid the groundwork for Celtiberian grammatical studies. His paper entitled "Las inscripciones ibéricas y la lengua de los Celtiberos" appeared in 1947 and included Celtiberian coin legends which were written in the Iberian script. This was the first conclusive evidence of an Indo-European language spoken in preRoman Spain.

In 1955, Michel Lejeune, in his book *Celtibérica* brought together much of the fragmentary information pertaining to the Celtic language of Spain, and Schmoll in his *Die Sprachen Der Vorkeltischen Indogermanen Hispaniens Und Das Keltiberische* (1959) synthesized the state of the art vis-à-vis linguistic aspects of the ancient Hispanic tongues.

Villaronga's essay "La evolución epigráfica en las leyendas monetales" (1958) was a pioneering study and summary of all Iberian and Celtiberian text and coin legends. Juan Malaquer de Motes wrote a text entitled "Epigrafía prelatina de la península ibérica" (1968) particularly for use of students as an introduction dealing with the history of Iberian writing.

At nearly the same time, Ulrich Schmoll in his monograph *Die Südlusitanischen Inschriften* (1961) and Gómez-Moreno in *La escritura Bástulo-Turdetana* arrived at the conclusion that the script of southern Portugal contained the same kind of inner form as the Iberian script even though the two approaches did not agree on details.

Coin legends in this region and corresponding classical citations of place names are not available, nor are corroborating inscriptions in Latin or Greek alphabets, and many of the transliterations are controversial.

Linguistic studies concerning all the known languages of preRoman Spain and Portugal were further elaborated on by Tovar in 1960 in the *Enciclopédia Linguística Hispánica* and in *The Ancient Languages of Spain and Portugal* (1961).

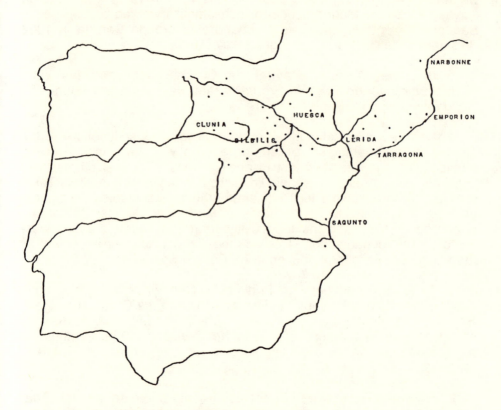

Map 3. **Iberian and Celtiberian Mints in northeastern Spain After Untermann (1975)**

Studies revolving around numismatics, place names, suffixes and personal names have been recently carried out by Faust, Palomar Lapesa, Albertos Firmat and others. Notable for their work in southern France are Soutou and Richard.

In 1975, Jurgen Untermann published his *Monumenta Linguarum Hispanicarum* Vol. I on Hispanic numismatics, incorporating photographs of the available coins and an analysis of their legends and locations of the mints. In 1980, Volume II appeared as an equally comprehensive study of the Iberian inscriptional material of southern France.

J. Hoz and J. Siles carry on important linguistic studies in a wide-ranging area of the ancient languages as well as Fleuriot, Schwerteck, S. Mariner, Oroz and others.

A recently discovered lead plaque written on both sides from Los Villares (Valencia) is one of a growing number of documents from this locality. The inscriptions and the transliteration proposed by Fletcher Valls[7] are as follows:

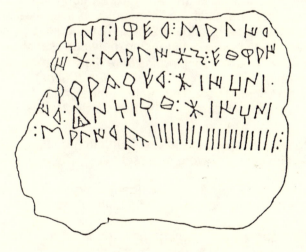

Fig. 7a Inscription from Los Villares

Fig. 7b Inscription from Los Villares

Side A

bilosiunteşalir [gan]
ega:ga IIIIIIIIIII elerte
ba:şalirbosita şalibos
ngantobanteinbeletene
iboeganteşalirga IIIIIIIIIII
dibandebaşalibosendenbilos
ştentiste:arabagi:bobaitinba
ganegaşalir:ga IIIIIIIIII
ba:iuntibilose

Side B

[bobai]tinba:barer:şalir
[bos]ita:şalirbos eterai
?aragarer:bobaitinba
[şal]ir:duntibarte:bobaitinba
:şalirga IIIIIIIIIIIIIIIIIII:

Fig. 7c. Transliteration of the Inscription from Los Villares (Valencia)

This inscription is indicative of the kinds of linguistic problems and perverse features encountered in the process of transliteration. The missing, worn away, or broken section of the tablet presents a problem with the beginning and ending of each line. Sometimes, as in line one, the sequences may be supplied if the context seems appropriate as in this case where *ganega* occurs elsewhere in the test. Such suppositions are not verifiable, however.

Other questionable features revolve around the sign Λ before the series of vertical strokes. Does it stand for an abbreviation or a word? Does the vertical stroke at the beginning of line three represent a syllable (*ba*) in word final position or does it represent a number?

Some sequences of signs are of great length, not interrupted by word boundary markers, such as lines four and five. Is *şalir* (line 5) one word as it appears to be on side B (line 1), or should it be considered as *şalirga*? And what is the relationship between *şalirbos* (line 3) and *şalibos* (line 6)?[8] The sequence *bilosiunte* (line 1) (*bilos-iun-te*) appears more or less reversed in line 9 *iuntibilos* (*iun-ti-bilos*). Is this syntactic arrangement significant to a relationship in meaning? The form *bilos* is a proper name elsewhere (compare the Bronze de Ascoli).

An interesting aspect of the text found in the first and last two lines is the apparent inversion of word order, cf.

bilos iunte şalir [gan]ega ga-
ganega şalir ga-ba iunti bilose

Is *iun* the same word or morpheme found on the Alcoy Lead tablet, i.e., in *iunştir*[9] or does *iunte* relate to the first part of *iunte gens* in the Cigarralejo lead? Do *iunte* (line 1) and *iunti* (line 9) represent simply

30

variants or are *te* and *ti* different morphemes? Does the document continue the same line of thought on the opposite side as it seems to?

Sequences such as *iunṣtir* (Alcoy) and *iumṣtir* (Ullastret), *baide* (Castellón, Alcoy, Mula, etc), *adin* (Ensérune to Andulucía), *ildir* (Lérida to Mogente) and many others demonstrate a degree of linguistic cohesion throughout. Some investigators see the same language spoken from the middle Guadalquivir and the Sierra Morena along the coastal regions to southern France.[10]

The dearth of Iberian inscriptions to the west of Obulco (Porcuna) in the region of lower Andalucía may perhaps be explained by the amplitude of Phoenician and Carthaginian activity from an early time and the use of the indigenous Tartessian language in this area.

FOOTNOTES

[1]Some hieroglyphic signs appeared in southern Spain imported from Egypt. See Maluquer 1968, p. 13 and Untermann 1975, pp. 69 ff.

[2]See Untermann, loc. cit. Some scholars see the orthographic system of the southwest as almost entirely of Phoenician origin, e.g., Javier de Hoz 1979.

[3]Untermann 1975 Text I, and 1984c. Along the lines of Gómez-Moreno, he treats Y as a nondescript nasal [m̄]. In a somewhat elaborate analysis, Siles 1981 gives it the value of [na], [a] and [n] depending on its contextual environment. See also Fletcher Valls 1979 for a systematic but inconclusive treatment of this sign and Beltrán Lloris 1974 for a brief history of views and problems associated with Y.

[4]According to Fletcher Valls Ϋ occurred once out of 850 repetitions of signs in the province of Castellón and six times out of some 800 on the ceramic inscriptions from San Miguel de Liria.

[5]For historical commentary on the transliteration of Hispanic writing, See Caro Baroja 1946 and Untermann 1975.

[6]*Ibid.*, p. 52.

[7]The plaque measures 104 mm in length and 80mm in width. Its original state was somewhat longer. From Fletcher Valls 1978.

[8] For examples of *şalir* in Iberian documentation, see Siles 1976.

[9]The form *inunştir* is attested 21 times in Iberian inscriptions, sometimes with [m] and sometimes without the nasal, i.e., *iustir*, see Untermann 1985.

[10]See Tovar 1961, p. 55.

Chapter 3

EASTERN IBERIAN INSCRIPTIONS

Documentary remains from the Levante and northeastern regions of the peninsula are the most numerous spanning at least five centuries with inscriptions from Emporion dating back to the fifth century, B.C., from the fourth century at Ensérune and Ullastret and coin legends from the end of the third and persisting into the first century, B.C.

Until the end of the third century, B.C., Greek coins minted at Rhode and Emporion circulated in the northeast. Transformations in Iberian society resulting in more sophisticated and expansive trade led to the minting of Iberian coins along the lines of the Greek models.

Along with coin legends and metal plaque engravings there were rupestrian inscriptions often relating to funerary stelas, and ceramic writings. Iberian coins were minted in a number of localities ranging from Obulco and Iliberis in the south (Andalucía) to Emporion and Ensérune in the north, including such modern-day sites as Huesca, Lérida, Mataró, Barcelona, Tarragona, Jativa, Azaila and others.[1] The numerous legends often refer to place, personal and clan names. Depending on the mint, the coins were issued in silver, bronze or copper and at certain locales the Iberian script was usurped by that of Latin or Greek.

**Fig. 8   Drawings of Iberian Coins
After Untermann (1975)**

Lead pressed into thin sheets was a common material for inscriptions throughout the Mediterranean basin and inscribed lead plaques were utilized in Iberian territory from the fourth century, B.C. to become more numerous in the subsequent centuries. The first lead inscription known was the Lead of Castellón discovered in the nineteenth century and now in the Museum of Archaeology in Madrid. More of these plaques at Emporion and Ullastret have appeared, as well as at El Solaig (Castellón), Liria, Orleyl (Valencia) from Andalucía and from southern France. In short, these documents are found in all regions of Iberian territory.

Transliteration:

ybardiaigis abarieigide sinebedin urgegerere aurunibeigeai astebeigeaie egariu adunin boduei baidesgi egusu sosinbiuru borberoniu gosoiu baidesgi berigarsense uldidegeraigase argidiger aigas balgebiuraies baidesbaniegarse

Fig. 9   Lead Plaque of Castellón and Transliteration
After Gómez-Moreno   (1949)   no. 43.

Discovered in excavations at Ullastret in 1967, the following lead plaque offers the sign ⚥ unique to this document and transliterated as be.

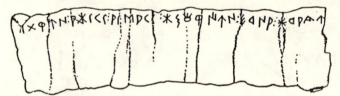

Transliteration:
        ar basiarebe
        ebarikame tuikesira borste abarkeborste ter . . .
        tirs baidesbi neitekeru borbeliorku timor . . .
        gir bartasko anbeiku baitesir saldukobakuleboberkur . . .
        bigildirste eresu kotibanen eberka boskalirs . . .
        lors abatibi biurbones saldugilerku ?
        batarun abobake abasakebe bosberiun erna borakau

Fig. 10   Lead Plaque from Ullastret and Transliteration
After Oliva Prat   (1967)

Note that Fletcher Valls transliterates Iberian Y as [w].

-ire:bododaṣ:bitebagirṣbane:baṛenyligi
  antinylirḍuṛane:ar̥ikaṛ:seken
-iuṣu:atilebeiu:lauṛiskeṛgate:
  banylirḅaiduṛane:kaisanylirḅaiduṛa:nei
-tailiniṛe:gudur:biteṛoketetine:
  eṛatiare:gogor:tauebartiate:
  ar̥ikaṛbinyligise
-iunstirlaku:bododaṣeai:selkeaibarduneai:
  unibeikeai:aneṛai:unibeikeai:iu
-nstirlaku:uskeike:bododigi:
  keietisiatense:uṣtalarikaune:
  banyiṛeṣu
-lu:bitiṛokebetense:uskeaneṛlati

**Fig. 11 Lead plaque from Orleyl (Valencia) and
Transliteration After Fletcher Valls (1981, p.64)**

The following lead inscription from the region of Valencia, damaged as many are from the Iberian practice of rolling them up like scrolls, contains signs superimposed over other signs. The form of the various letters, both in style and size indicates more than one scribe. A phonetic rendition of the text presents numerous difficulties except for some sequences already identified on other documents. No transliteration is given here.

**Fig. 12   Lead Plaque from Yátova (Valencia)
After Fletcher Valls (1980), p. 26**

A copy of an inscription on lead, found in 1949 in the temple of Asclepius at Ampurias (Emporion) appears in Figure 13.

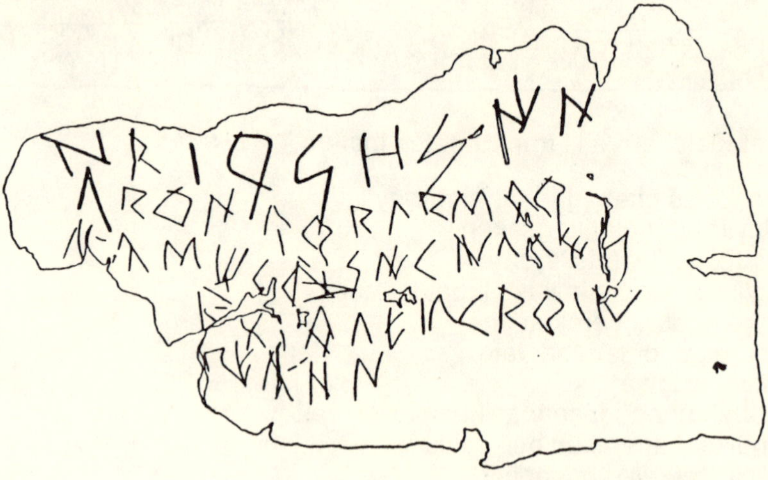

Transliteration:

nabaṛsosin
lagunuṛalaṣkar
okaṣtikersikenṣtis
aṛbakalebalkeaṛban

aelon
sikounin
ilakotinebabon
abaṣkaduṛabanui

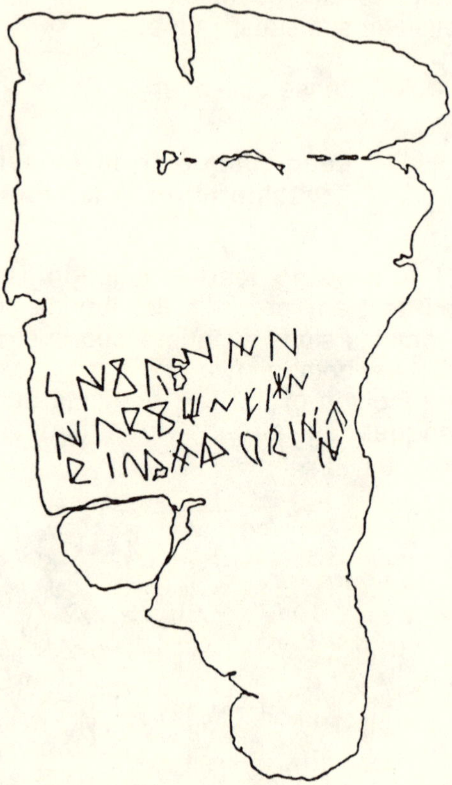

**Fig. 13   Lead Plaque from Ampurias and Transliteration
After Maluquer (1968), p. 228**

Of frequent occurrence are inscriptions on ceramic materials that may have been stamped during fabrication, or at some point incised or painted, a process that applied to both indigenous and imported wares. An important group of these ceramic inscriptions comes from the Iberian town of Liria whose pottery is in the style of its Greek precursors and whose inscriptions seem to complement the painted scenes as explanatory commentary of the themes represented. The writing offers a clear tendency toward a cursive writing that contrasts in some cases with the rigidity of the orthographic signs of monetary legends.[2]

Fig. 14   Inscribed Vase from Liria
After Gómez-Moreno   (1949)

Fig. 15   Ceramic Inscription from Liria
After Maluquer EPPI, p. l2l

Also from Liria comes a pottery fragment with a decoration of battle, animal and fishing motifs along with an inscription whose second sequence of signs appears in transliteration as *kakuekiar*.

**Fig. 16 Battle and Fishing Scene from Liria
After Beltrán Villagrasa   (1942)**

By comparison with other inscriptions, a single sequence of signs on a vase or bowl sometimes represents a personal name, perhaps the owner of the ceramic in question. For example.

ᛕᐱᐃᐸᑭᛘᛀ

ilduradin

**Fig. 17a Ceramic Inscription from Azaila and Transliteration
After Cabré, p. 24**

Other times, only a letter or two is given implying an abbreviation or potter's mark.

ᛁᛉ ↑ᛁ ᐱ ᛁᛉ ᛈ

**Fig. 17b   Ceramic Inscription from Azaila
After Cabré**

Ceramic material offers a broad chronology of Iberian writing and language insomuch as the inscribed piece can be dated to a specific century or epoch.

More difficult to date are inscriptions on silver plates or goblets. Cf.

Transliteration: bateirebaikarsoginbaikar

Fig 18. Inscription incised on a silver receptacle from the Iberian village of Tivassa (Tarragona) and Transliteration.
After Maluquer (1968), no. 238

Inscriptions were incised on grave stones and cippi reflecting Roman influence and are especially prevalent from Emporion, Tarragona and Sagunto, all focal points of Roman interest. From Tarragona (ancient Tarraco) various inscriptions contained both Iberian and Latin words. Other sites of Iberian stone documentation are found throughout Catalonia in Lower Aragon, the Valencian region and southward into Murcia. Most of these inscriptions seem to belong to the first and second centuries, B.C. Some perhaps, are a little older and a few others a little later.[3] The orthography is the same as that employed on coins.

Transliteration: areta
　　　　　　　ineba
　　　　　　　eildu

Fig. 19 Stone Inscription from Sagunto (Valencia) and Transliteration
After Gómez-Moreno (1949)

Of unusual design is a tombstone found four kilometers to the south of Cretas on which were engraved five lances. If Aristotle was correct in saying that the Iberians planted a lance around the tomb for every warrior killed by the deceased, here we have a more permanent presentation of this act of commemoration.

Transliteration: kalun seltar

**Fig. 20   Stone Inscription from Cretas and Transliteration
After Gómez-Moreno   (1949)   No. 24**

Discovered in 1941, a stone inscription from Sinarcas, reasonably clear in most aspects, contains a somewhat unusual first line or heading:

Transliteration:

baisetaṣitudaṣeba[
nyiseldarbanyi
berbeinarieugia
]yikatuekaṣkoloite
kaṛieugiarseldarban
yibasibalkarybaṛyi

**Fig. 21   Gravestone from Sinarcas and Transliteration
After Gómez-Moreno   (1949)   No. 76**

40

A sandstone inscription, discovered in 1939, has endured in legible form except for along the upper edges where some letters were obliterated.

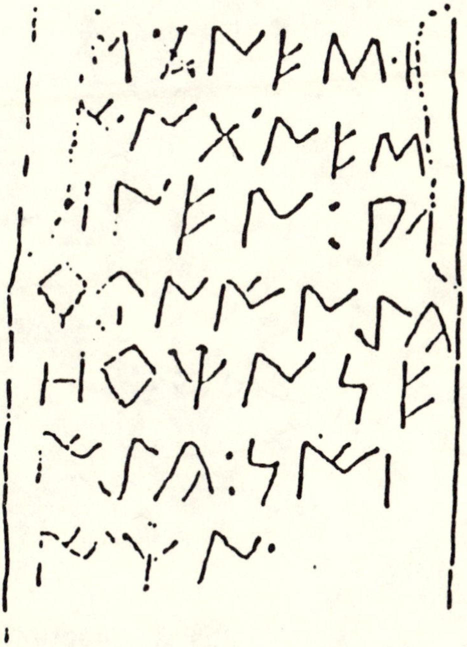

Transliteration:

]ṣkoneṣ[
]intaneṣ[
ebanen:au
ṛuninkika
oṛtinse
ikika:siba
itin

Fig. 22 Stone Inscription and Transliteration from Santa
Perpetua de la Moguda
After Gómez-Moreno (1949) No. 15

Inscriptional material relating to the broad zone designated as Iberian shows enough lexical similarity to suggest close linguistic affiliation, if not one general language, among the ancient peoples. Similarly, grammatical and morphophonemic features seem to link the areas together linguistically.

41

Map 4. Iberian Inscriptional Sites

The linguistic structure of the language also remains decidedly obscure since without some semblance of meaning, the relationship of words and morphemes can only be analyzed on a purely distributional basis. Iberian, for example, shows the following sequences:

> ba
> bai
> bais
> baise
> baiser
> baisetas

Such forms suggest a case-structured and somewhat agglutinating language not unlike that of modern Basque, cf.

[gison]	'man'
[gisona]	'the man'
[gisonaren]	'of the man'
[gisonarentsat]	'for the man'

42

Another example of what appears to represent a derivational process in Iberian morphology occurs in the sequences:

$$
\begin{array}{llll}
\text{ba} & \rightarrow & \text{ba-r} & \rightarrow & \text{ba-r-i} \\
& & \text{ba-s} & \rightarrow & \text{ba-s-i} & \rightarrow & \text{ba-s-i-r} \\
& & \text{ba-n} & \rightarrow & \text{ba-n-i} & \rightarrow & \text{ba-n-i-r}
\end{array}
$$

The arrows signifying 'becomes' are only relevant if the forms are grammatically related -- a still unknown factor.

Note that what seems to be a stem *ban* in conjunction with a morpheme (di) among the words *bandi*, *diban* and *banidir* is further complicated by the fact that one cannot be certain whether or not the sequence *di* in *banidir* is the same *di* in *bandi*, i.e., *ban-i-di-r,* or relates to the sequence *id* as in *ban-id-ir* in which *di* → *id* when the ending *-ir* is added. The language contains innumerable, and so far inscrutable, examples of this type.

Seeming related pairs of words such as

gani	gadin
gari	gadir
gasi	gadis

could be constructed on allomorphic stems *ga-* and *gad-* or an infixal morpheme {d} could institute a phonological readjustment in which *ni* becomes *in* after a consonant. Other possibilities, of course, exist.

A major problem in Iberian studies is the difficulty in penetrating the morphological structure even within purely distributional parameters, a matter which precludes a broader comprehension of the syntax. In the sequences *aredage* and *agedebane* note the apparent reordering of phonological units, i.e., *edage* and *agede*. Are these somehow related words? Is *age* a morpheme and *de* or *ed* another?

Without knowledge of the meaning we cannot know if *ed* and *de* are recorded sequences of the same morpheme, independent units, or simply phonological sequences devoid of semantic content.

Ullastret

Lying in an area of rolling hills in northeastern Catalonia, ten kilometers from the Mediterranean Sea and thirty meters above the surrounding land, the Iberian town of Ullastret, still well preserved in broad outline, offers an absorbing impression of Iberian life. The walls and towers partly surrounding the town made up one of the most impressive fortifications of ancient indigenous architecture. The houses inside the town were generally rectangular and often had more than one room, with walls of dry stone and floors generally of clay with little or no special decoration. Paved floors of flagstone or pebbles were rare. Many had benches along one wall, at least one fireplace, and a smoke outlet in the roof. Silos or granaries nearby were bored out of the bedrock of the hill as were the cisterns, the largest of which had a capacity of about 150,000 litres.

The site of the town was sporadically occupied since Upper Paleolithic times. By the third millennium B.C. occupation was fairly intense. But the first stable settlement relates to the transition period of the Bronze to Iron Ages toward the end of the seventh century B.C.

After about 575 B.C. the first Ionic ceramics appeared, along with Etruscan amphora. The oldest Attic vase of black figure style, a kylix, is dated to about 536 B.C. During the second half of the fourth century, quantities of ceramics appeared which were very similar to those of the southeastern peninsula, suggesting commercial relations with Iberians along the Mediterranean coast.

Ullastret was already a populated center when the Greeks founded Emporion, a few miles north on the Bay of Rosas, and while close contacts existed between the two, Ullastret did not lose its autonomy at least until the beginning of the fourth century as indicated by a vigorous indigenous material culture, although both Punic and Greek influence was present. Life in the town probably enjoyed its greatest splendor during the latter years of the fifth century, B.C. and the first quarter of the fourth. During the fourth century, however, a fire destroyed much of the town.

From the beginning of the third century, B.C. a decline set in due perhaps to the growing importance of nearby Emporion in whose orbit Ullastret now stood. The town was abandoned early in the second century, B.C.

Inscriptions in the Iberian language have been unearthed at Ullastret on ceramic material and on small thin lead plaques. At least one inscription was in Punic writing and another in Greek, but generally the native Iberian prevailed.

In artistic endeavors, the Iberians concentrated primarily on sculpture and painted pottery. Sculptured pieces were produced in stone, bronze, and baked clay and were used as offerings in the sanctuaries or as funeral tokens. Human simulacrum such as the famous *Dama de Elche,* inspired perhaps by Greek models, reached a high degree of perfection. Animal figures represented both the objective world of horses, bulls, and lions and symbolic or mythological creatures such as were known in the eastern Mediterranean.

44

Iberian pottery from the sixth century, B.C. appeared with painted horizontal bands or lines, and later with circles or half circles and other themes in geometric patterns. Still later these themes were supplemented by decorations of vegetable motifs and eventually by a cross section of Iberian life depicting dancing, horse taming, and battles, as well as animals - fish, eagles - often in some kind of metamorphoses. In short, Iberian pottery decorations progressed from stylized curves to illustration of flora and fauna and finally to baroque forms between the sixth century, B.C. and Roman Imperial times.4

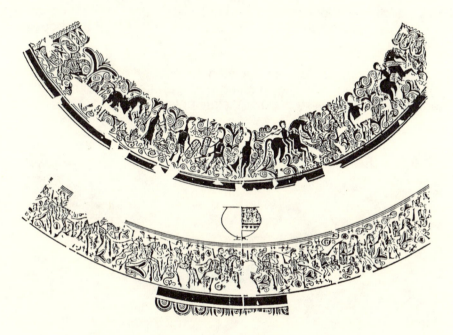

Fig. 23   Pottery Decoration from Liria
After García y Bellido (1980)   Fig. 146

Certain aspects of Iberian social organization are evident in their extant art, architecture and to a lesser degree from statements of classical authors. The independent cities of the Levante and Catalonia appear to have lacked a monarchical tradition, and it may be supposed that they were often at war with one another which would account for the rise of a skilled warrior class. The art of war and its participants were often depicted on Iberian ceramic paintings. The Vase of Warriors from Liria, for example, exhibits foot soldiers and cavalry engaged in combat. The warriors wore short tunics, a kind of scaly armor and helmets; they carried circular shields, javelins and falchions. From the sixth to the end of the third centuries, Iberians served under the command of Carthaginians and, at times, in the service of the Greeks. In various

45

military undertakings they were quartered sometimes in Sardinia, Sicily, Greece, Italy and North Africa. Later, they were enlisted as mercenaries by the Romans.

The Hispanic peoples were skilled horsemen able to supplement their supply of animals from the abundant wild horses on the peninsula, and at least one sanctuary (El Cigarralejo) was dedicated to the worship of a horse goddess.

Among other aspects of ritual, a pottery fragment from Elche displays a winged goddess attributed to Hellenic tradition and connected with dove worship in which the bird personified the mother goddess of fertility.

Iberian daily life is also depicted on pottery scenes illustrating a fondness for music, dancing, hunting and warfare. The flute and long saxaphone-like horn were popular instruments.

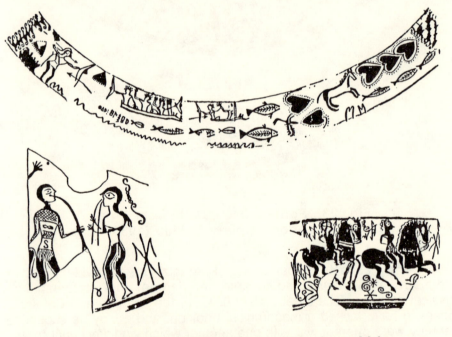

**Fig. 24   Iberian Pottery Decoration from Liria
After García y Bellido (1980) Figs. 149,
150, 151**

Iberian women had a flair for personal adornment, from ornate brooches to earrings. They often dressed in long-sleeved, belted tunics

46

down to the feet. The mantle was also a highly decorated article of clothing worn like a poncho and secured by a waist belt.

Somewhat at odds to the manner in which Iberians painted themselves, the Romans considered them austere, hardy and savage. In reference to the Lacetani of Catalonia, Livy describes the tribe as "deviam et silvestrem." However, the Iberians were more civilized than the Romans cared to admit since they sometimes fought against the legions as well as for them. In the realm of agriculture, they cultivated cereals as well as the vine and olives, the latter items introduced by the Greeks.

Sheep, oxen and pigs added to the Iberian range industries and fish produced from sea and stream supplemented their diet.

Southern France

The earliest writing in ancient Gaul was introduced by the Greek colonists who founded Massalia (Marseilles) around 600 B.C. At about the same time, Iberian-speaking people appeared north of the Pyrenees, attracted there no doubt by the richness of the land and opportunities for trade along the coasts. Their towns were not situated on the coasts directly, but near enough to participate in the sea trade and to be astride the land trade routes between Italy and Spain. The Greek colony at ancient Agde ('Aγαθη) at the mouth of the Herault river, is thought to have been the direct trading partner of the Iberian towns in southern France. Around 400 B.C., the Iberians of this region acquired the skill of writing which apparently derived from Iberian territory and towns to the south.[5]

The largest number of inscriptions from southern France are in Iberian writing on ceramic material which occasionally contains several personal names, but more often, just one name. Many of these inscriptions end in Yi which is thought to mean something like 'belongs to,' or 'I belong to.' Often added directly to the name were the syllables *en* or *ar* or *aren* which could be a case suffix, perhaps with a genitive or ablative function.

Some engravings are simply pottery marks: two are on stone and during later times, four were inscribed on lead plaques at Pech Maho. There is very little variation among Iberian orthographic symbols from the Valencia-Alicante regions to southern France. A few minor differences are the I₹ - shaped sign for the sound [a] instead of ⋈ or ⋈ and the sign ⅄ . for [be] instead of ♉ or ⋈ . The reading of the sign ⅄ found in France and at only one mint in Spain is still unexplained.[6]

Iberian settlements and inscriptions are found at sites such as Mailhac, Montlaures, Chateau Roussillon, Pech Maho, Elne and

Ensérune, the latter, the best excavated and the type site of an Iberian society, spread out over southern Gaul during the first and second phases of the Iron Age.

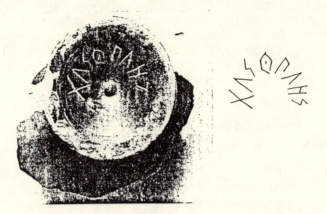

**Fig. 25   Iberian Inscription from Southern France
After Untermann (1980)**

The populations of these towns spoke and wrote the Iberian language about 400 - 100 B.C.   Iberian inscriptions have also been found at other places such as Lattes, La Lagaste and Aubagnan further west, although the documents in question could have been transported to these sites where Iberian communities may not have actually existed.

One inscription in the orthography and style of southern Spain offers some testimony to distant connections among the Iberians of France. As typical of Andalucían documents it reads from right to left as follows:

ЧІ?+Ч7Z   (kilutaṛu)

The Iberian orthography and language may have been the only one readily available to serve the local needs as a written or spoken lingua franca and thus was employed as such as a writing system for non Iberians. Non Iberian words and names are evident in the inscriptions and in order to piece together a coherent picture of the linguistic influences that contributed to the Iberian language and culture, it is necessary to determine to which language group belong the non Iberian names mentioned in the inscriptions.

The identification of Iberian names in France can be facilitated by comparison with those found on inscriptions in Spain and with the names on the Ascoli Bronze, but sometimes phonological characteristics of the

48

Iberian language tend to be violated among certain names, suggesting that these were not of Iberian origin.

Gaulish names are identified with more certainty than other non Iberian names as they are known from Latin sources. More difficult is the identification of names of Ligurian provenance which are less numerous. Others unknown, perhaps pertained to small undefined ethnic groups and languages of the vicinity.

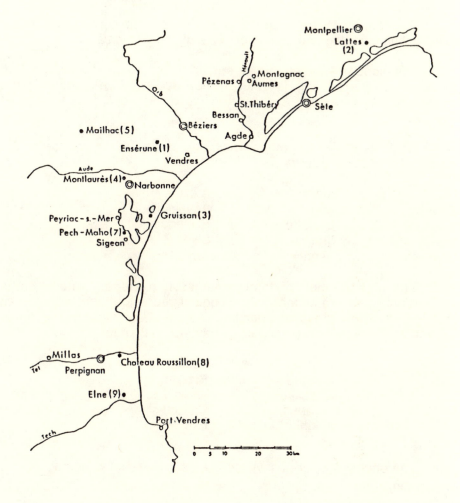

Map 5. Iberian Settlements in Southern France
After Untermann (1980)
(Inscriptional sites marked as . and numbered)

49

When confronted with non Iberian words, scribes employing the Iberian script had to resort to certain strategies in order to render the word in Iberian. To handle combinations such as *tl* and *br*, clearly not conducive to the Iberian syllabary, another syllable was required, cf.

Iberian Name	Presumed Origin
anetilike	Anextlikos ?
kabiṛilo	Cabril(l)o ?
balante	Blandus ?

The Iberian syllabic sign appears chosen to contain the same vowel as the following one, i.e., *ti, bi* or *ba*, cf. *tili, biri, bala.*

The scribal manoeuvers seem to substantiate the notion that occlusive sounds + [r], [l], [s] and [n], non occurrent sequences in the alphabetic texts (Alcoy, Ascoli, etc), were indeed a fact in Iberian phonosyntactics.

Other examples of names which seem to have run counter to the Iberian phonological pattern are:

ateto	Atexto ?
auetiṛiṣ	Advectirix ?
eṣkinke	Excingus ?
tiuiṣ	Divix ?
aṣetile	Adsedilus ?[7]

The incorporation of foreign names into Iberian, affecting the orthographic and presumably phonological representation, would also theoretically show signs of adjustment to Iberian grammar. Latin or Gaulish names in *-us* or *-os* appear to have *-e* in Iberian:

aṣetile	<	Adsedilus ?
balante	<	Blandus ?
anetilike	<	Anextlikos ?
kaṛate	<	Carantus ?
eṣkinke	<	Excingus ?

The ending *-ius* or *-ios* yielded *ie* as in *kobakie < comagius* ? or sometimes just *i* cf.

luki	<	Lucius ?
tiberi	<	Tiberius ?
korneli	<	Cornelius ?[8]

In short,

Iberian		Latin/Gallic
-e	<	-us/-os
-ie, -i	<	-ius/-ios

The name *eşkinke* has a parallel in Basque [eskin/iskin] from the stem *is-* meaning 'a chatty or loquacious person.' Similarly, the name *anaios* (*anaios arenyi* pottery inscriptions from southern France), which appears to have been incorporated into Iberian without a change in the desinence resembles Basque [anai] 'brother,' cf. also [anaioso] 'brother of father or mother.' A Basque variant is [anaie] 'brother' the expected Iberian form from *anaios*.

Iberian inscriptions in southern France pertaining to the second and third centuries, B.C. are especially numerous but so far there is no clear evidence to connect the Iberians of the Narbonne region to those of Spain by a specific Iberian invasion into Gaul. An Iberian *Bevölkerung* into southern France has not been established by archaeological evidence apart from cultural similarities and inscriptional material purporting a common language.

Coin inscriptions from the area indicate that purely Iberian legends were issued by only some mints. The word (place name) *neronken* was common but on Latin coins appeared in conjunction with the official name *tiuiş* which seems to have been a Gallic proper name, i.e., *Divix*.

Another mint employed Iberian writing but Gallic names-- *birikantin, birikantio*, while yet another inscribed the names of local tribes in Greek orthography and language. The mint of the town *Baeterrae*, seemingly an Iberian name, located only a few kilometers from Iberian Ensérune, used exclusively Greek letters.[9]

During the period of the preRoman coinage (200-50 B.C.) the region of western Narbonensis appears to have been under the sway of Gallic political power and the use of a common Greek writing in opposition to Iberian orthography, while Iberians, Gauls (Celts), Greeks and Ligurians cohabited the area. From a cultural perspective, based on inscriptions and ceramics, Iberian settlements in southwestern Narbonensis and Catalonia appear similar. The sites in both areas indicate a tendency toward an ordered town design with rectangular street patterns which, from earlier reliance on the natural configuration of their hilltop locations for defence, developed stout walls. Iberian towns, however, seem to have been only sparsely fitted with the things one would expect for full urban activity such as market places, public buildings and temples.

Iberian peoples seemed to have dwelt in southern France as far east as the Rhône river, beyond which, according to ancient authors, lived Ligurians of unknown affinities. Linguistic evidence that could be used to substantiate the ancient claims is extraordinarily meager, consisting of a few local names and glosses, but the possibility of a few loan words from Ligurian to Iberian is not out of the question. The word *biu*, for example, in Ligurian *biu-elius*[10] (Greek Βιος) 'life', Latin *uiuus* 'alive' and Iberian *biur* in the names *biurbones, biurno, biurbi, biurbiken, biurtibas, biurtetel, biurtite*, indicate similarities that seem more than coincidental.

Ensérune

The hilltop site of Ensérune, one hundred twenty meters above the surrounding plain and fifteen kilometers from the Mediterranean coast is one of the most productive for Iberian documentation, yielding to date 371 inscriptions of which more than a third can be identified as names.[11] The original designation of the town is unknown; the name occurred for the first time in medieval documents of the tenth century in the form of Anseduna, a name which may have been close to the original and whose final part is reminiscent of Celtic -*dunum* 'hill'.[12]

Under the north slope of the hill once ran the via of Heraclea, the preRoman road from Italy to Spain. Near the south slope lay another ancient road. Both connected the town of Narbonne with the local villages and with the port of Agde (then Agathe) with Marseilles further east, and the lower Rhône valley.

The occupation of the site has been dated from ceramic material, the earliest of which appears to have been Etruscan and Greek (Ionian and Attic) and which fix the date of the initial settlement between the fourth and sixth centuries B.C. Compared to other local indigenous sites, notably Mailhac, Ensérune appears to have been occupied relatively late. It was abandoned during the first half of the first century A.D. During the course of its inhabited existence, the town was partially destroyed (by Celts?), was rebuilt, and adopted the practice of incineration, presumably through Celtic influence.

Undoubtedly of commerical importance, the town may well have been established as an outpost or go-between for the Greek products entering Massalia (Marseilles) and the Celts of the hinterland. The first occupants of the hill, confident no doubt of the commanding height, neglected to construct protecting ramparts.

The population of the town consisted of autocthonous Iberian peoples who were perhaps in the region from earlier times, and of invaders, Hallstadt carriers of the Urn Culture, who occupied the surrounding plains about the ninth century B.C.

Unlike other coastal towns such as Massalia, Agde or Emporion, there is no evidence that Ensérune was ever a Greek city. The original ethnic populations, dominated by Iberians, persisted throughout the life of the town and continued many of the traditional cultural features.

Hellenic, Celtic and eventually Roman influence added to the character of the town. A Celtic aristocracy seems to have superimposed itself on the population and later Roman writers mistakenly uniformly called the people they found there, Gauls. Iberian traditions persisted, however, to the last phase of the town as evidenced in the continued use of the Iberian language inscribed on ceramics. The written documentation is attested from the beginnings of the fourth century, B.C. or the end of the fifth, by numerous examples. It is reasonable to suppose that the Iberian language was employed at Ensérune and surrounding sites before it was committed to writing. Greek and Latin inscriptions at Ensérune were very rare and Iberian seems to have endured as the primary language of the town even for a time after the Roman conquest.

Fig. 26 Pottery Fragment and Inscription from Ensérune
After Untermann (1980)

The demise of Ensérune was apparently due to relatively stable conditions in the region under the *Pax Romana* where the disadvantages of living on a narrow, crowded hilltop, especially with the constant effort to obtain water, finally gave way to an orderly move to the plains. The inhabitants appear to have left little behind. The Iberians and their language finally succumbed to the Romans and the Latin language which came to constitute in Languedoc the Gallo-Roman culture.

Pech Maho

Twenty kilometers south of Narbonne was situated the small town of Pech Maho founded in the sixth century, B.C. and abandoned in the third. At the site several lead plaques have been found in various states of preservation and containing a few doubtful signs, e.g. ⊕ , ⊟ , ⅄ . Apart from some variations, the script is Iberian and much of the vocabulary corresponds to that of inscriptions south of the Pyrenees.

Fig. 27a   Inscription from Pech Maho
After Solier (1979) p. 78

The first half of the inscription in Figure 27a, keeping in mind that some signs are problematic, reads:

eisburebal [?]
bakaṣketaisureṣ
tiniṛ: baiteskike
noroboṛ : atinbuṛ
ikei : kuleṣkere
bastike ; leisir : bilos
tibaṣ : tikirsbin :
bortuoṛiṣ : baṣbin : bokalṣ
or : atine : beleṣbaṣ :
arsbin : kanbuloike
bakaṣketai : kiskeṛbon
eṣuṛesuniṛ :

Fig. 27b   Transliteration of Inscription from Pech Maho

The sequence *buṛ* as in *atinbuṛ* appears to have been a variant (dialectal?) of *biur* in the name *Atinbiur* on inscriptions in Spain. Similarly, the words and personal names *ban, abars, adin, baites, beles, bilos, iltir, kules, sani, tibas, tiker,* and others from Pech Maho inscriptions are common in documents from Ullastret, Emporión, Castellón, Liria and El Solaig.

FOOTNOTES

[1] See Untermann 1975 for a complete collection and analysis of Hispanic coins.

[2] Fletcher Valls 1953.

[3] Maluquer 1968, p. 67.

[4] For Iberian art, see García y Bellido 1980, and Nicolini.

[5] Greek pottery of the later seventh century, B.C., has been found in the vicinity of the mouth of the Rhône river in the native villages of Saint-Blase and La Couronne. After the defeat of the Greek fleet at Alalia in 535 B.C. at the hands of the Carthaginians, Hellenistic influence underwent a hiatus only to re-emerge around 400 B.C. with a new

influx of Greek ware into the western Mediterranean. This period corresponds to the first Iberian inscriptions in southern France and northern Spain. The earliest datable texts are on red-figured Attic ceramics. A little later the so-called Campanian receptacles from Greater Greece appeared which were the dominant style of cultural artifact in the western Mediterranean for the next two centuries.

[6]For an authoritative collection and study of inscriptions from southern France, see Untermann 1980.

[7]For these examples, *Ibid.*, pp. 47 ff.

[8]*ibid.,* p. 48.

[9]*Ibid.*, p. 43.

[10]For Linguistic evidence of Ligurian, see Pulgram 1978, p. 35.

[11]At Azaila on the Ebro River in Spain, 541 different graffiti have been unearthed but only 70 of them consist of more than two letters, and only 20 offer complete names. Liria with 84 and Ullastret with 55 are also prolific sites for Iberian inscriptions.

[12]Perhaps Anceduna, 'hill of Ance', as suggested by Untermann 1980.

Chapter 4

SOUTHERN PENINSULAR INSCRIPTIONS

The majority of southern Iberian documents have come from the eastern section of Andalucía and the upper valley of the Guadalquivir, extending roughly from Abenjibre and the river Júcar, westward to Porcuna (or the ancient capital of Obulco in the province of Jaén) and Córdoba. Celtic penetrations may, in part, account for the dearth of inscriptions in the western part of the province. Similarly, early Romanization may have been a factor in the early disappearance of the epichoric writing. Italica, near Seville, was the first Roman city in southern Spain founded in the year 206 B.C.

The transliteration of the southern Hispanic script remains far from resolved and offers few of the guarantees established for the phonetic values of the northern Iberian inscriptions.

The influence of the Phoenician writing system in the south of Spain, however, is patent. Signs are too similar to be coincidental, but enigmatic details persist, for example, the sign $\triangle$, is closest to Greek *alpha* and not Phoenician $\mathcal{K}$.

The area was seemingly a zone of intermingling and contact between Iberians, Celts from the meseta, Tartessians from further west, Semites from North Africa and the eastern Mediterranean, and Greeks.

Andalucían epigraphic remains are not uniform but show a mixture of traditions. They appear as a kind of transition zone between the Iberian to the north and the southern Portuguese script, presenting a somewhat imprecise epigraphical boundary to both. Southern writing was generally from right to left, more in accordance with Punic tradition than with Greek but similar to that of the earliest Greek writing for which are extant examples. While agreement on the southern peninsular phonetic values is far from unanimous, a composite sketch of the signs and plausible values is presented below.

Vowels	$\triangle$	$\triangleleft$	[a]	
	$\ddagger$	$\bar{\top}$	[e] ?	[o] ?
	$\nearrow\!\!\backslash$		[i]	
	$\otimes$	$\diamond$	[o] ?	[e] ?
	$\sqcup$		[u]	
	$\uparrow$		[?]	

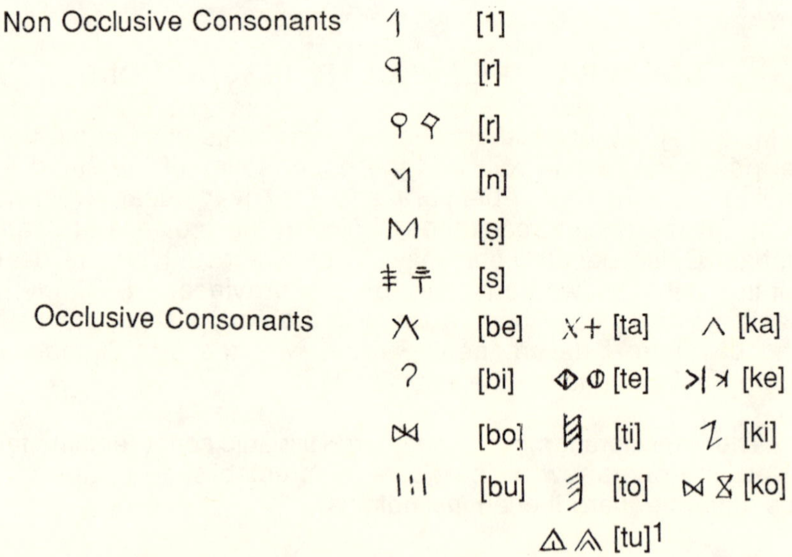

Non Occlusive Consonants	ʎ	[1]				
	ꟼ	[r]				
	ꟼ ꟼ	[ṛ]				
	˥	[n]				
	M	[ṣ]				
	‡ ╤	[s]				

Occlusive Consonants	⋋	[be]	Ж+	[ta]	⋀	[ka]
	?	[bi]	◆ ◑	[te]	>⏐ ⼈	[ke]
	⋈	[bo]	⅄	[ti]	⅂	[ki]
	⼁⼁⼁	[bu]	⋹	[to]	⋈ ⋊	[ko]
			△ ⩘	[tu][1]		

Othographic similarities to northern Iberian have prompted corresponding phonetic values whose representations are often not verified, however linguistic parallels with northern Iberian seem to occur in the vocabulary of the southern inscriptions. For example, a coin legend from Obulco reads ˥◆ꟼꟼ◆ʎ˥ and has been interpreted as *ilderaden* where both *ilder* and *aden* are found in northern Iberian documents (see Ascoli Bronze).[2]

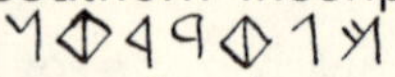

Coins from ancient Obulco, with engraved sprigs of wheat, ploughs, and yokes, etc. reveal the agricultural aspect of the town. In Andalucía coins again offer some clues to the transliteration of signs, for example, the legend ⋀ʎ ⼁⼁⼁ ⋋ has been read as *ibulco* by Gómez-Moreno (equating ⼁⼁⼁ with [] [bu]). He also interprets the coin legend ˥◆⩘ꟼ⋊ズ⋋ as *iskeraten*. From another site, Cástulo, now Cazlona (Jaén), Iberian coins have been discovered, one of which carried the inscription ‡ʎ◆M⋀ read by Gómez-Moreno as *castele.*

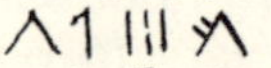

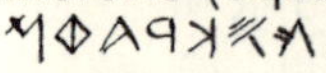

Coins from southern Spain belong primarily to the second and first centuries B.C. and were minted in several places. From Cástulo, some coins were engraved with the image of a wolf and a legend something like *ileraka,* evocative of coin inscriptions from Ilerda (Lérida). Some from Obulco contain the names of magistrates in Latin, e.g., L. Aimil (L. Aemilius) and M. Ivni aed (M. Iunius aediles). Others show the name of the city or Iberian magistrates. Coins from ancient Iliberis, (Roman Municipum Florentinum Iliberritanum), (Granada), bear the legend *Ilberiṛ Kestin* or simply the first word ⊢ �⋏ ⋀ ꟼ ⊢ ꟼ (where ꟼ = [ṛ]. Coins minted at Urci [urki] show riders in the northern Iberian style and legends such as *urkeṣken.* Still other inscriptions from unknown mints end in *sken*, an ending characteristic of northern Iberian monetary legends, cf.

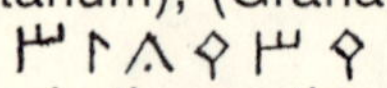

ᴎΛᴦOⱯkᴎ (*ikalosken*). Legends in Roman script appear to originate at Abra, a site not yet identified.[3]

The oldest Andalucían documents appear to be contemporary with the oldest northern Iberian inscriptions such as those from Ullastret and Emporion and written on lead plaques of the fourth century, B.C.

Entering this area from the east, one of the first sizable texts that comes to the attention is the Mogente Lead Tablet written in the fourth century, B.C. Many of the signs coincide in form to Iberian but not all. The horned *lambda* ᴎ , as well as Ⱨ and ᵻ and Ч , were not employed in the Iberian zones but are found on the southern Portuguese inscriptions.

This lead tablet contained a comparatively extensive text but appears to have been mainly a chronicle of names, at least on one side.[4] It was conceivably a dynastic record but little more can be said since what ostensibly are names, have not been identified.

This document, as well as any, exhibits the discrepancies of transliteration among Andalucían signs. Compare:

	Tovar	Baroja	Maluquer	Gómez-Moreno	Schmoll
Ⱨ	to	e	u	e	o
φ	be	r	r	ku	r̩
⋈	bo	ko	ko	bo	ko
ᴎ	ku	ba	be	be	?

Based primarily upon the transliteration of signs by Gómez-Moreno, the word *saldula* in the Mogente text is reminiscent of the word *salduie* found on the Celtiberian coins of *salduba* and of the word *salduti* inscribed on a vase from Liria.[5] One might also compare **saldui-* reconstructed from *sallui-* on the Ascoli bronze tablet. Similarly, the

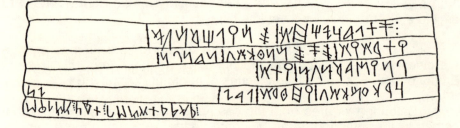

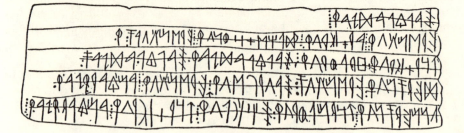

Fig. 28a   Lead Plaque from Mogente
after Maluquer (1968)   p. 133

etalaukititobe sioldiŗikan
otarbeobe sesinkukebeka nanbin
binoşaŗikan otabe
urkekuikebeka otokurbe lagi
şolibe uduta bişibetarakar

plus the repetition of the following words on the reverse side:

şaldulako	- kia ŗ
	e
aiduar?	- kiaŗ
toŗsibe	- ka ŗ
	aeŗ
	e
arta	- ker-kaŗ
uorta	
koldiş	- tauten
burlder	-
botorei	-
sakarbiş	- kaŗ
kanitoren	-
stikel	-

Fig. 28b   Transliteration of the Mogente Lead Tablet

word *sakarbiṣkaṛ* ⴼ⋀Ⲙ⛭⋀◁‡ seems connected with *ṣakariṣker* on both the lead tablet of Liria and that of Alcoy. The lead tablet from Mula contains *sakarbis.*[6]

Compare also *sesin, toṛsibeka* and *tauten* on the Mogente lead and *sosin, torsinno* and *tautin* on the Ascoli bronze. The sequence *urke* of Mogente also occurs elsewhere, e.g., on the Alcoy and Castellón lead tablets.[7]

The controversial nature of the signs, however, render comparisons of the language with those of other areas something less than convincing. The sequence ⴼ⋀ⵝⵦⵏⲘ◁ⵊ (first word, second line, side A) written right to left, has been variously read as *erṣibakaṛ, erṣikukabe, erṣibekaṛ,* and *torṣibekaku.*

The difficulties confronting the linguist or archaeologist when dealing with inscriptions from the southern region of Spain are exemplified by the Gádor lead tablet, discovered in 1862 in a silver mine in the Sierra de Gádor (Almería). There is little common ground among the divergent opinions concerning the transliteration of this document. Not only is the phonetic transcription of some of the signs problematical, but also in several cases the signs themselves are questionable and have led to conflicts in copying them. Seemingly unique to this inscription are certain configurations such as ⟨ and ⱶⴵ , the latter perhaps a stylized form of Ⲙ [n].

**Fig. 29   Drawing of Gádor Lead Tablet
After Tovar (1961) p. 51**

As the signs resemble those of the Obulco monetary inscriptions the plaque is thought to date to the second century, B.C.

The text appears to have been a record or an account perhaps of the quantity of ore extracted from the mine as represented by the vertical lines at the end of each lineal sequence.[8] Transliteration of the inscription has been varied and diametrically opposed inasmuch as at least one investigator read the document from left to right, while others have read it from right to left. The southern Portuguese ᛐ and Iberian as well as Andalucían ↑ are all found on the inscription and present problems in transliteration. Cf.

	Gómez-Moreno	**Maluquer**
◇	o	ku
ᛐ	u	o
↑	ü ?	u

Following Maluquer's transliteration, the text reads:

.dukuro tui tecus śtari etesu
bisku uleşkes śtari etesu
ego uleşkes śtari etesu

---

ego uleşkes śtari etesu[9]

On the other hand, a reading by Gómez-Moreno appears as:

uduoruduinomstarienmü
bisteüleskemstarienmü
ecoleskemstarienmü
enüleskemstarienmü[10]

There is possible Latin influence in the forms *ego, tui* and *tecus* suggested by Maluquer (a plausible deduction considering the fact that the document has been attributed to the second century, B.C.) but this is, at best, questionable since a definitive reading is not available.

From other Andalucían sites have come inscriptions of various kinds. A few are on lead plaques, a number are in the form of coin legends, and a fair collection of inscriptions are found on silver utensils such as platters.[11]

The inscriptions engraved on silver receptacles are difficult to date with any precision but appear to come from early Roman times on the peninsula, or a little before. The most impressive are those from Abengibre, several of which are presented below.

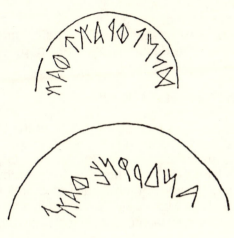

**Fig. 30   Inscription on Silver Receptacles from Abengibre
After Gómez-Moreno   (1949 & 1962)**

Other silver receptacles or platters have been discovered at Torres, Padraz, Fuensanta de Martos and Santiago de la Espada.

A very few inscriptions from Andalucía were engraved on stone such as one from La Alcudia de Elche, transcribed as *atekubeiaterko* by Gómez-Moreno and *ateiriaterko* by Maluquer. Another, less clear stone inscription was discovered by 1903 at El Salobral a little south of Alicante.[12]

Phoenician-based writing but with vowels and other alphabetic signs may well have been introduced into the region of the lower Guadalquivir in the vicinity of Cádiz or Huelva, and adopted by the inhabitants of the ancient kingdom of Tartessos. It is feasible that as the script spread to the east and northeast, crossed the Júcar and entered the Levante, it came under strong Greek influence radiating from Hellenic centers along the coasts. Under Graeco-Iberian influence, the system became more uniform and more Hellenized. It would appear more than coincidental that as one enters the Iberian zone the direction of writing changes in accordance with Greek traditions, certain signs disappear from the texts. while other, more distinctively Greek, were employed.[13]

Similarities of signs, of the direction of writing and style indicate cultural affinities between Andalucía and southern Portugal but linguistic relationships underlying the documentation are apparently more closely linked to northern Iberian,[14]

Libya-Phoenician (Turdetan) Writing

From the end of the second century, B.C. in the region of the lower Guadalquivir, local towns employed a system of writing on coins completely distinct from Iberian or Andalucían Graeco-Phoenician writing. It has been labelled Libya-Phoenician or Turdetan and was used primarily among the cities west of the Straits of Gibraltar. The cities and towns to the east, such as Malaca (Málaga), Sexi, and Abdera employed a pure Phoenician system to record the Phoenician language.[15]

**Map 6. Location of Libya-Phoenician Mints
After A. Beltrán**

64

The coins inscribed with the Turdetan signs were also imprinted with the name of the mint in Latin which greatly facilitated the identification of the cities that employed this type of script, namely Arsa, Asido, Bailo, Iptucci, Lascuta, Oba, Turricina, and Vesci - all situated in the limited area between Gibraltar and Cádiz. The orthographic system was as follows:

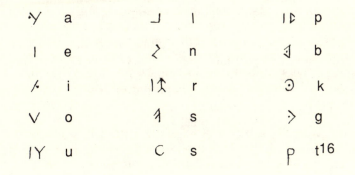

·Y	a	⌐	l	ID	p
I	e	ζ	n	⧢	b
⁄·	i	⫯	r	Ɔ	k
V	o	⫴	s	⟩	g
IY	u	C	s	P	t[16]

Map 7. Southern Hispanic Place Names
After Untermann (1984)

The manner of writing seems to have been alphabetic. The limited number of signs and their partial resemblances to those of other orthographic systems, for example Greek and Phoenician, reveals little about the origin or chronological development of the script. Resemblances to Old Libyan, although not consistent in phoenetic values, have suggested to some scholars that the writing and even the language were Libyan, compare Old Libyan ⊡ [b], ∨ [š], | [n], ⊃ [m], ℂ [s].[17] The facts of the matter are, however, that the origin of the script and the language underlying it remain in the realm of speculation.

While the language of the southern inscriptions appears to be the same or a dialect of northern Iberian, albeit with some differences in the orthographic traditions, there are, however, clearly some very different linguistic features in the south - features not found in the northern areas such as the names of towns in *ip(p)o* and *-uba* in delimited areas that extended into southern Portugal.[18]

FOOTNOTES

[1]Some investigators have given ✝ the value of [o] and ◇ that of [e]. The sign for northern Iberian ↑ sometimes occurs on the same Andalucían text as ⊣ (even juxtaposed), cf. Mogente Lead. Schmoll reads ↑ as [u] and ⊣ as [o/u]. The sign ⏉ is assigned the value [r̩] by Tovar, Maluquer and Schmoll but [ku] by Gómez-Moreno.

The phonetic value of the sign ⋋ interpreted as [be] by Gómez-Moreno is far from certain. |:| read as [bu] by Gómez-Moreno is given the value [bo] by some scholars.

The letter ⟁ read as [te] here has also been read as [ti]. Gómez-Moreno read ⬖ as [tu] and ⋀ as [du]. The only place a voiceless/ voiced contrast was made. These and many other differences of opinion regarding phonetic values characterize the southern Iberian inscriptions.

The values are here generally but not entirely based on those given by Gómez-Moreno 1962.

[2]See Gómez-Moreno 1962, p. 63.

[3]*Ibid.*, pp. 62.63. For the above references to Andalucían coins and mints.

[4]The inscription measures 180 x 49 x 1 millimeters.

[5]See Gómez-Moreno 1962, p. 58.

[6]*Loc. cit.*

[7]For some similarities between lexical forms linguistically connecting northern Iberian and southern Iberian zones, see Tovar 1961, pp. 53ff.

[8]The document measures 175 millimeters wide, 110 high and 2-3 thick.

[9]Maluquer de Motes, 1968, p. 46.

[10]Gómez-Moreno *Ibid.,* p. 46.

[11]See Gómez-Moreno *Ibid.,* pp. 51-4 for these and other inscriptions of this type.

[12]See Gómez-Moreno *Ibid.,* p. 55 and Maluquer *Ibid.,* p. 80.

[13]Modifications to the script perhaps have a parallel in pottery styles which were introduced by Punic traders in the initial phases of contact in the south of Spain, but underwent changes as they spread and entered areas under Greek influence. See Cuadrado pp. 257-90.

[14]For a concise history of investigations into Andalucían inscriptions and orthography, see Hoz, 1976.

[15]The designation Libya-Phoenician is somewhat misleading for two reasons: the Libya-Phoenicians (or Blastophoenicians) cited by classical sources inhabited the coastal area east of the Straits to about as far as Almería; neither the script, nor the language have been definitively shown to be Libyan or Phoenician.

[16]After a good deal of investigation of the signs of numismatists, they were established to the satisfaction of many scholars by Beltrán, 1985. See also Maluquer de Motes, 1968, p. 107. A few scholars who have worked on the problem are Zobel de Zangroniz, Meinhof, Schoeller, Zyhlarz, Gómez-Moreno, Vives and Tovar.

[17]For Libyan signs, see Jensen, p. 155.

[18]Based on place names that have persisted in spite of early latinization of the south and on information recorded by classical authors. See Untermann 1984.

Chapter 5

SOUTHERN PORTUGAL

With abundant deposits of silver, tin, and copper, southern Portugal constituted one of the early anthropic focal points of the peninsula. The populations of this region which included the Algarve, the Alemtejo, and Lower Extremadura maintained among themselves internal relations in the commerce of metals, and, as might well be supposed, carried on contacts with eastern societies. But the degree of liaison and interdependence between these broad linguistic and cultural areas is still a matter of conjecture.

With the Phoenician colonization of Gadir[1] and other southern localities, leading to more intensive mining operations to supply the eastern Mediterranean markets, urban centers appeared whose increasing wealth attracted still more people. Celtic tribes from the

Map 8. Inscriptional Sites of Southern Portugal

interior, for example, penetrated the southwest cultures to become part of the ethnic make-up of the regional population.2 By the sixth century, B.C., Greek influence was added.

Here, in the southwest corner of the peninsula, we enter into a new zone whose eristic documentation has not been adequately penetrated. While the orthographic tradition employed in southern Portugal seems related to Iberian writing conventions and practice, the phonetic values of most signs remains virtually unsubstantiated by external confirmation. Presumed underlying phonetic values based upon obvious counterparts in Iberian, Phoenician and Greek participate in distributional arrangements that point to a unique and so far unrelated language.

The inscriptions in the style and language of the extreme southwest have been found as far east as Alcalá del Río (Seville) and Villamanrique de la Condesa (Seville). The first exists only in a copy, the original having been lost. The second, a fragment, was discovered only recently.

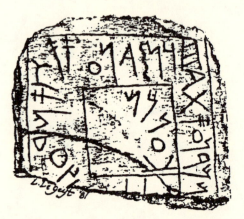

Fig. 3l   Drawing of a Typical Southern Portuguese Inscription

The script employed throughout the Algarve and Alemtejo appears to date from the fourth to the second centuries, B.C., judging from the similarities of the signs with southern monetary legends, although opinions differ.

The retrograde manner of writing approaches the boustrophedon style with the signs placed around the edges of the stone, following its rectangular contour, the foot of the sign directed toward the center. Word boundary markers were not employed in these inscriptions, while the

70

stones themselves generally underwent little artistic elaboration, appearing as if they had just come from the quarry. These documents display a good deal of uniformity in both script and content.

The majority of the Portuguese inscriptions so far unearthed were written on stone slabs and appear to have served as grave markers, although most were redeployed for material in later tombs, sometimes with the inscription facing inwards, its significance perhaps no longer relevant. Consequently, they are often not associated with their original site and function.

An interesting feature of the inscriptional language centers around the distribution of vowels. Syllabic signs, if indeed the writing system was syllabic or semi-syllabic, were often followed by non syllabic vowel

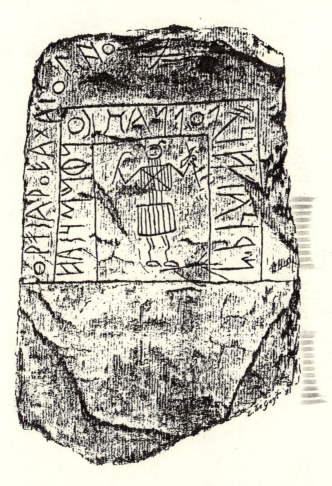

Fig. 32 Southern Portuguese Inscription with Scribe

signs which were equivalent to that designated by the syllabic symbol, so that sequences such as *kaa, kee, kuu,* etc. were common. Schmoll[3] maintained that this represented a notational device to signify the presence of long vowels. There is currently no way to substantiate this proposal.[4]

Writing in this region was restricted to tombstones with the exception of coins from Salacia (Alcacer do Sal). Few ceramic inscriptions and no lead plaques have so far been uncovered. The available texts, often repetitious and formulaic, suggest a pietistic orientation or perhaps a kind of magical incantation for the dead, and in this sense they were probably inscribed under the direction of a restricted religious group or priestly cast. Unlike Iberian, writing in this area did not seem to be an affair of the ordinary citizen.

The signs of the writing system and their phonetic values were thought to be essentially the same as those for Andalucían but the disagreements over phonetic values that plague Andalucían documents occur compounded among the southwestern texts.

Based on the table of phonetic correspondences presented by Maluquer (1968) the southwestern script appears as:

∧	[a]	1	[l]	ᐤ	[r]
‡	[e]	ᴎ	[m]	φ	[r̩] ?
ᵛ1	[i]	ᴎ	[n]	⅗	[s] ?
⨆H	[o/u] ?	Ɔ	[?]	M	[ś] ?
↑	[u]			‡	[ṣ] ?

plus syllabic signs:

∣	+	∧
⋎Υ	Φ ⋈	⟩∣
?	⋹	⋏
✳	H Ⴒ	✕
☐	△ ∧	○

Others interpret the values of the signs differently, suggesting one type of [r], two instead of three sibilants (where ⸲ = [m]) and so on.

Controversy over the syllabic or alphabetic nature of the Portuguese inscriptions dates back at least to Hübner, the eminent collector of ancient Hispanic documents who, in his *Monumenta Linguae Ibericae* put numerous documents at the disposal of investigators and pronounced the script to be alphabetic. Schulten, working with the data, followed the same course, identifying the signs and the language to his satisfaction. He perceived the language as Etruscan and equated the Tartessians of Tartessos, that is, of southern Spain and Portugal with the Tyrrheni (the Greek word for the Etruscans) who Herodotus said came originally from Lydia.5

According to Schulten, the script was brought to the peninsula by early migratory proto-Etruscan colonists before Phoenician or Greek sailors arrived in the western Mediterranean. Accordingly, these Etruscan-Tartessians occupied Andalucía, initiated the building of the monumental sepulchres or dolomites and reached a stage of metallurgy producing gold and copper and specialized ceramics which were carried throughout Europe.

Schulten had observed that a sequence of signs found on some of the Portuguese inscriptions seemed to be similar to a sequence on the Lemnos Stone, discovered in the locality of Kaminia on the island of Lemnos in 1885 and which was considered to belong to the sixth century, B.C.

Fig. 33 Lemnos Stone
After Pedersen, p. 219

73

Inscribed on the stone is the sequence ΙΑΥΟ9ƎΖ transliterated (from right to left) *zeronai.* The striking resemblance of this word to the Tartessian sequence ΑΥΟ9ΑΖ read as *sarona* or *zarona* gave Schulten the clue he needed to equate Tartessian and Etruscan since the Tyresenos or Tyrrhenos were considered to have inhabited Lemnos as well as southern Thrace and Italy.[6]

Schulten's judgment that the writing was alphabetic was supported by the signs such as ΥΥΥΟϞ which appeared to relate to the Koni, a people of the Algarve referred to by ancient authors along with the existence of several cities such as Konistorgis and Konimbriga.

While Schulten's views were generally accepted at the time, no progress has been made to equate further the two languages of Tartessian and Etruscan. Following the efforts of Gómez-Moreno who pronounced the southwest writing to be semi-syllabic (analogous to Iberian), attention has now generally turned away from the idea of an alphabetic system and from Etruscan origins.

For Gómez-Moreno, the best evidence of the semi-syllabic nature of this script lies in the fact that the system contains twenty-eight signs, more than necessary for an alphabet (although this is debatable) and less than required for a full syllabary. The number of signs is comparable to the Iberian system. Along with Gómez-Moreno, others, for example Schmoll and Caro Baroja, also reached similar conclusions concerning the type of writing although not necessarily the individual transliterations.

Compare the readings of the stela in the museum of Figueira da Foz (actually discovered at Bemsafrim):

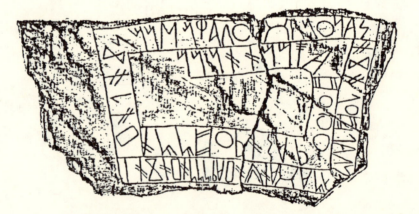

Fig. 34   Funeral Stela From Bemsafrim Portugal and Transliteration

74

Transliteration:

Schulten	ieqeoniiraoeeahainil alolequesaronahkoiao isiinqeleoeiionaesarao asiieenii
Gómez-Moreno	lecoobuoniirabuedue abeairicaaltiolecoenan onabekeonacuisiincoe lebueiitioremaroteo tiasiieeenii
Schmoll	okooponiirapooVoaaia ikaalHelokoonanenaea piisiinkoolopoiHeros areeeHasiioonii

Schulten and Gómez-Moreno agree generally on the vowels and continuant consonants, or about ten signs in all, while they differ in about sixteen signs. Gómez-Moreno and Schmoll agree on the syllabic nature of the writing system but have very little else in common.

According to Maluquer, the first word of Gómez-Moreno's reading should be *baeco* instead of *leco* and probably pertains to a personal name. Maluquer, for example, suggests that the sequence *baeco ebueni* means 'Baeco, son of Ebueni.' Some of these names appear related to the onomastics of the region: *Ebueni* suggests the name of the Eburones, a people known to the southwest from the sixth century, who have left their name in the toponymy, e.g., Evora.

Characteristic of the southwest funeral inscriptions is the ritualistic expression 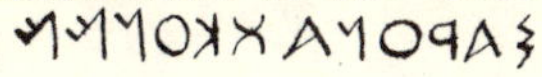 transcribed here as *saronabekeonii*.[7]

A comparison of these sequences found in the various documents (whatever the definitive transcription may look like) reveals features that could be associated with inflecting type languages in which grammatical forms are added to a stem to make up larger sequences, cf.

keo
keoni
keonii
keondei
keondeir
keono
keonai

The sequence ‡ 🯅 (*bue-*?) seems to correspond to distributional features not unlike *keon-* with regard to presumed suffixes. Its separate morphological status is assumed by the following sequences:

Ɣ Ƨ ‡ 🯅   (buegin?)

ꟼ Ɣ ‡ 🯅   (bueir?)

‡ Λ ‡ 🯅   (budue?)

Ɣ ‡ ˥ ‡ 🯅   (buelen?)

ꟼ Ɣ Ɣ Ɣ ‡ 🯅   (bueniir?)

The abundance of vowel combinations of the language of the southwest presents a striking contrast to other areas of the peninsula. Sequences of two, three, four and perhaps even five vowels occur in the texts, cf.

ꟼ Ꮞ Ꮞ Ɣ Ꮞ ⊢ O ‡ ... (sotiuiuur?)

In the southwest, no proper names have yet been clearly identified notwithstanding the funerary nature of most of the inscriptions. In spite of some reasonable assessments of the relationship between signs and phonetics, of word and morpheme boundaries based on combinatory analysis, the language remains obscure, untranslated, and apparently, with present knowledge, unrelated to any other language, ancient or modern.

FOOTNOTES

[1] In preRoman times the Bay of Cádiz was larger and contained two islands: the greater of the two was called Gadir (Greek Gadeira, Roman Gades). Ancient sources place the foundation of the site by people from Tyre in the eleventh century, B.C.
  Archaeological support for this early date is lacking, but Gadir was clearly flourishing and under Phoenician hegemony by the eighth century, B.C.

[2] The existence of Celtic elements in the lower region of Guadalquivir

accords with Avienus' account of Celtic penetrations into the region of the Tartessians and Gades in the sixth century, B.C. See Arribas, p. 45.

3Schmoll, 1961.

4For other possibilities, see Hoz, 1977.

5Herodotus states that the central province on the western coast of Asia Minor, Lydia, was the native land of the Etruscans. The Greek name of the Etruscans, Tyrsenos or Tyrrhenos, points to Asia Minor, for the Greeks used the suffix *-enos* only with Asiatic names. They were mentioned in Greek sources as inhabitants not only of Italy but also of early Athens and the island of Lemnos.

6It might be noted here that an ancient Hurrian god who occupied an important place in the onomastics of Asia Minor in the second millenium B.C. was called *šaruma,* a word not far removed in structure from the southwest inscriptions. One document from Asia Minor reads **muua šaruma* and can be compared to Tartessian *maon sarona.* This god was assimilated into the Luwian pantheon, see Houwink, p. 136.

7Note the various transliterations of this sequence.

Gómez-Moreno	maronabekeonii
Schmoll	šarena⋈keenii
Maluquer	sarkunabekekunii
Tovar	saronabekeonii

Chapter 6

HISPANO-CELTIC LANGUAGES

A major change in the cultural and linguistic panorama of the Hispanic peninsula which affected large areas, especially in the north, occurred in the initial phases of the first millennium, B.C. New types of villages and burial rites appeared, along with metallic and ceramic elements unknown in Spain and Portugal until that time. This abrupt break with the older traditions by new religious manifestations, new cultural artifacts and, presumably, by new linguistic habits (all of which were similar to those employed in western Europe) can thus be related to the arrival in Spain through the Pyrenean passes of the Celts.

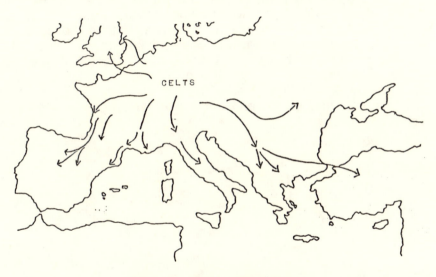

Map 9   Celtic Migrations

This new population has been identified from reports of contemporary Roman and Greek historiographers (mostly in connection with their resistance to Roman hegemony), from archaeological remains, from toponyms, and from inscriptional material. Part of this group, the Celtiberians, left behind comparatively extensive documentation relating to land and property distribution, funeral inscriptions and coin legends. In the west and northwest of the peninsula the inscriptional material is less plentiful, however, while the central plateau regions seem to have been generally devoid of written documentation.

The Indo-European nature of the languages spoken by these people is clear from Celtiberian inscriptions, one of which reads in part:

TVROS   CAROQVM   VIROS   VERAMOS

The word *turos* in the nominative singular, appears to be a personal name of someone who belonged to the clan (*gens*) of the *Caroqum*, a form in the genitive plural, and was a man (*viros*) of supreme qualities as judged by the word *veramos* which has been equated with Indo-European **uper*, cf. Greek *úper-*, Sanskrit *upari*, but showing in Celtiberian the typical loss of Celtic /p/.[1]

The Celtiberians were an aggregation of Hispano-Celtic peoples who occupied the eastern portion of the central meseta. First cited in the third century, B.C. by Polybius and Livy, they soon after gained a reputation as fierce warriors in the wars against Rome.[2]

From the Roman point of view, Celtiberia was a poor region of uncompromising harshness which was nevertheless rather well populated by various Celtic tribes. The most numerous of these were the Arevacos, an agricultural people who were situated on the slopes of the Upper Duero and inhabited such towns as Numantia, Agreda and Segontia (Sigüenza) in the vicinity of present-day Soria. Some Celtiberian towns were discovered from their ruins while others are known from coin inscriptions and from statements of early writers, but with sites still unidentified.[3]

1. Arevacos
2. Belos
3. Lobetanos
4. Lusones
5. Olcades
6. Pelendones
7. Titos
8. Turboletas

Map l0.   Some Celtiberian Tribes

In dealing with the Celtiberian language and documentation, we find ourselves in more familiar territory. Words and suffixes can be compared to other Indo-European languages and especially to known Celtic languages of the Indo-European family. Often, the meanings of the words and endings through such comparisons become discernible.

Coin legends denoting place names with equivalents in Latin or Greek have greatly contributed to an understanding of Celtiberian and it is clear that it was spoken in the regions of the modern provinces of Soria, Burgos, Logroño, Guadalajara, western Teruel, Zaragoza and southern Navarre.[4]

Fig. 35. Celtiberian Coin Inscriptions from Untermann (1975)

These Celtic populations who settled in the territory of the eastern meseta developed contacts with the Iberians of the central and upper Ebro, such as the Ilergetes and the Edetanos, and borrowed, amongst other things, the Iberian orthographic system to record their own language.[5]

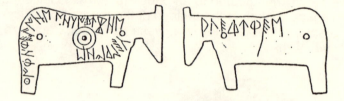

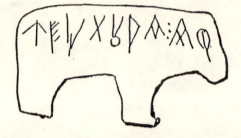

**Fig. 36. Celtiberian Bronze Tesserae in Iberian Script[6]
After Gómez-Moreno (1949) no. 82, 97**

Contemporary with the use of Iberian orthography Celtiberian tribes also employed the Latin alphabet. Both systems were first utilized in the second century, B.C., although documentation in Latin seems to have been less extensive than that making use of the Iberian signs.

**Fig. 37. Celtiberian Inscription in the Latin Alphabet
After Maluquer (1968), p. 143**

The orthographic signs taken over from the Iberians underwent a modification in the relationship between sign and sound, i.e. the Celtiberian $\mathcal{N}$ = [m] and Y = [n], the latter with a nasal quality it may also have approximated in Iberian), compare

ΜΧ⁄ΜΙ⧩Ν ΗΜ   [şegişameş]

With regard to phonological and grammatical features, the Celtiberian language seems to have preserved the archaic Indo-European labio-velar sound /kʷ/ lost, for example, in the Celtic languages of Great Britain. The preservation of this complex phonological unit appears in Hispanic names such as *Equabona, Equosera, Aquae Querquernae, Arquius, Equaesus,* etc.[7] Similarly, the semi-consonantal /y/ appears to have occurred in the words *Belaiocun, Araianom* and /w/ in *Deiuoreigis.*[8] The consonantal system for Celtiberian may be schematically presented as follows:

-	t	k	kʷ
b	d	g	-
m	n		
	s		
	l		
	r		
w		y[9]	

The reduction of Indo-European /-kt-/ occurred in Celtiberian. The name of a Numantian hero, *Retugemo* or *Rhetogenes* corresponds to *Rectugenus.* The form *Reitugenus* is attested in Gaul.[10]

The archaic Indo-European features of Iberian Celtic are evident in the preservation of diphthongs, of which the proto-language was thought to have contained at least six:

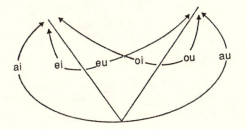

ai   ei   eu   oi   ou   au

The glides [ai] and [au] occurred in Classical Latin, while the others, prior to their merger with long vowels, occurred in early Latin. For example, *deico > dīcō, douco > dūcō.* Celtiberian seems to have contained all six original Proto-Indo-European diphthongs although *eu* often appeared as *ou.*[11]

In contrast to other Indo-European languages, Celtic stands out for the loss of the sound /p/, the process having taken place as /p/ > /f/ > /h/ > ø, compare Latin *pater,* Greek πατηP, Gothic *fadar,* and Irish *athir* 'father.' In some specific environments, the reflex of Indo-European /p/ was /x/, cf. Latin *septem* Irish *secht* 'seven' in which the process seems to have been /pt/> /ft/ > /xt/ in Celtic.[12] In some Celtic languages the sound /x/ was vocalized as is evident in Middle Welsh *seith.* The phoneme /p/ of Indo-European origin seems to have suffered a similar fate in Celtiberian, judging from its absence in inscriptions recorded with the Latin alphabet.

In 1908 a number of inscriptions were found engraved in the rock on Mount Peñalba in the vicinity of Villastar in the province of Teruel which were for the most part Celtiberian and written in the Latin alphabet. One of the texts reads:

> eniorosei
> uta tigino tiatunei
> trecaias to lugeui
> araianom comeimu
> eniorosei equeisuique
> ogris ologas togias sistat luguei tiaso
> togias

Based on comparative studies of Celtic and other Indo-European languages, the Celtiberian inscriptions have yielded a partial declensional system, although some case forms are still controversial. The word *luguei* in the above inscription appears to be a dative singular form referring to the Celtic god *Lug* (Irish *Lugh* or *Lug*), marked by the ending *-ei.* Lending credence to this interpretation is the word *to* considered to be a preposition 'to' (German *zu*). The ending *-om* in *araianom* has been taken to be an accusative singular desinence attached here to the compound form *ara* 'cultivated' and *ian* perhaps 'land,' (i.e., cultivated land or field). The endings of the words *ogris, ologas* and *togias* have been analyzed as accusative plural morphemes with *ogris* perhaps related to Latin *ager* (cf. Latin dative/ablative plural *agris*).

The morpheme *-o* as in *tigino* has been regarded as a nominative singular marker of a consonantal stem, as a dative singular, and as a genitive form. Other Celtiberian case marking morphemes are thought to be -*os* for the nominative plural, and a dative/ablative plural in -*ubos* or *ebos*. Some typical suffixes are -*ko, -iko, -tiko* and the enclitic -*que/-kwe/* 'and' as in *equeisuique* above, cf. Latin -*que.*[13]

Verb forms are fewer and less readily identifiable in Celtiberian than nominal elements, In the above text, *comeimu* clearly seems to be a verbal form, however, and has been analyzed as *kom-mei-mu*, a first person plural built on the root *mei* with the prefix *com-* and the first person plural marker -*mu* (compare Latin *com-* and -*mus*).[14] Similarly, the word *sistat* has been considered a reduplicated form of a root *sta* and a third person singular present tense verb again not unlike Latin third person singular verbs, cf. Latin *sto*. It could also be cognate with Latin *sisto.*[15]

The inscription reads along the following lines:

einorosei	-*ei* first person sing. 'I dedicate' ?
uta	'accordingly'
tigino	genitive singular ? }
	} 'to Tiatum of Tigno'
tiatunei	dative singular }
erecaias	accusative plural 'enclosures'
to	preposition 'to'
Lugeui	dative singular 'to Lug'
araianom	accusative singular 'land, cultivated field'
comeimu	first person plural 'we bestow' (recommend)
eniorosei	'I dedicate' ?
equeisuique	dative singular 'and I dedicate to Equeisui'
ogris	accusative plural 'fields'
ologas	accusative plural 'gardens'
togias	accusative plural 'coverings (sheds?)'
sistat	'offered' ?
Luguei	'to Lug'
tiaso	genitive singular 'of Tiaso'
togias	'coverings (sheds?)'

Some further cognate forms from Indo-European languages are:

Tigino	Tigurinus in Gaul
erecaias	*peri-cai 'around field' (note loss of *p*-) Welsh *cae* 'enclosed field (originally fence or hedge)' (see Buck p. 489).
araianom	Gothic *airþa* 'land', Irish *air-* 'plow, cultivate,' Latin *arāre* 'to plow,' and *ian* 'land' Welsh

85

comeimu	*llan* 'enclosure,' earlier 'piece of land,' Irish *lann*, English *land*, etc. (see. A. Macbain). cf. the Sanskrit root *mah* 'bestow.' Latin *com co-* and *-mus*.
equeisui	* ekµo? 'horse' ?
togias	Latin *toga* 'cover,' Celtic *togi* (Basque *toki* 'place,' *tegi* 'enclosure, shed') Greek *tégos* 'roof.'

Besides brief documents in copper, bronze, stone and ceramic materia others of a more substantial nature have been discovered in th Celtiberian regions such as the Luzaga Bronze written in Iberia orthography in the first century, B.C.

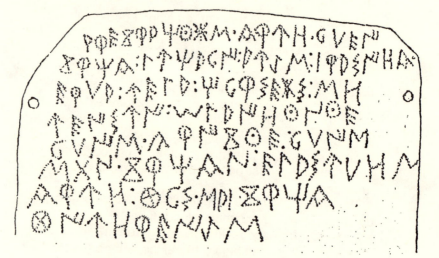

arekoratikubos karuo kenei
kortika lutiakei aukiş barasioka
erna uela tikersebos şo
ueisui belaiokumkue
keniş karikokue keniş
ştam kortikam elasunom
caruo tekes şa kortika
teiuoreikiş16

Fig. 38 Luzaga Bronze and Transliteration

The document is a kind of *tessera hospitalis* or token of hospitality like many other Celtiberian inscriptions.

The inscription of Botorrita, found in excavations near Zaragoza, is so far the most important document of this genre for its length and relatively complex syntax.

Somewhat difficult to read in places due to the ravages of erosion, parts of the document have been reconstructed to give a rather impressive array of sentences.

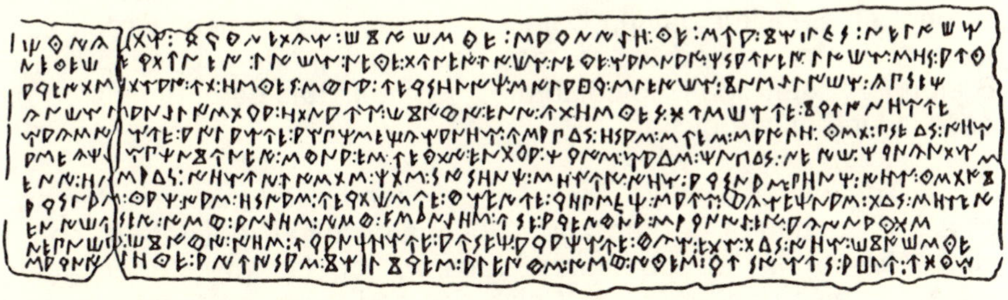

Transliteration:

tiriṣ[:]com.bercunetacam:tocoitoṣcue:ṣarnicio:cue:ṣua:combal ces:
ne litom
necue uertaunei:litom:necue taunei:litom:necue:maṣ nai tisaunei:
litom ṣosaucu
aretubea
otamai:uta:oṣcueṣ:ṣtena:ueṛsoniti:ṣilabuṛ:ṣleitom:consciliti
teurase cu
cantom ṣanciliṣtrara:otanaum:tocoitei:eni:uta:oṣcueṣ[:] bouṣtom-
ue:corui(:)some-ue
macaṣi(a)m-ue:ailam-ue:ambitiseti:camanom:uṣa bitus:osaṣ sueṣ:
ṣairo cuṣta:bisetus:iom
aṣeṣti:(a)mbitincounei:ṣtena:eṣ: ueṛtai:entaṛa:tiṛiṣ:matuṣ: tinatu(s):
neito tiṛi cantam
eni:oiṣatus:iomui:liṣtaṣ:titas sisonti:ṣomui:iom:arṣias:bionti:iom
cuṣtaicoṣ
arṣiaṣ:cuati:iaṣ:osiaṣ:ueṛtatoṣ-ue: temei-ue:robiseti:ṣaum[:]
tecametinaṣ:tatus:ṣomei
eni tousei:iṣte:ancioṣ:iṣte:eṣancios:use:aṛeitena:ṣarnicioi:
acainacuboṣ
ne bintor: tocoitei:ioṣ:urantiom-ue:auseti:aṛatim-ue teca(m)e com(:)
tatus:iom:tocuitoṣ-cue
ṣaṛnicio-cue:aiuisaṣ:combalcoṛeṣ:aleiteṣi: steise tae:i(u)simus:
abulu:ubocum[17]

**Fig. 39. Hispano-Celtic Inscription from Botorrita
and Transliteration**

Although there is disagreement among authorities concerning particulars, for example with the literal translation of some of the vocabulary, the Indo-European nature of the inscriptional language is manifest from the structure and the lexical forms. Compare *Acainacubos* "for the people of Acaina, for the Acainoi;' *ambi* a prefix 'around;' *areitena* comparable to Irish *aired* 'field' and Breton *aredenn* 'furrow, row;' *cantom* 'hundred,' cf. Latin *centrum; combalces* (com-balke) 'strong' (perhaps here in the sense of confirmed or guaranteed, seemingly cognate with Gaulish **balakon* and built on the root **balk* 'strong' cf. Sanskrit *balin-, bala-* 'strength' and ancient Greek *beltion* 'better;' *litom* related to the root **lei* cf. Irish *lith* 'good omen' and Breton *lid* ; 'fete,' *lidan* 'to celebrate;' *ne litom* has been translated *nefas esse* a kind of interdiction.

The words *sarnicio* and *sarnicioi* appear to have been the names of a god, although perhaps here the name of an obligation, compare Hittite *šar-nin-k* 'to substitute;' *taca(m)* or *daga(m)* 'good' may be related to Irish *dag-, deg-* or Welsh *da,* and *tocoitos, tocoitei* have also been taken to be the name of a god. *Usa* seems to mean ;high; and related to Irish *os, uas,* Welsh *uch* and Cornish *ugh* 'above, over,' etc.

To account for certain place names in Spain and Portugal and their apparent relationship with those of central and eastern Europe, theories of migrations, of diffusion, or of a general widespread Mediterranean substratum have all had their adherents. Many Hispanic names are clearly Celtic, however, and their occurrence outside the peninsula can be attributed to Celtic migrations as, for example, the appearance of the words *briga* and *dunum* throughout western Europe. Betanzos from Brigantium and Munebriga from Mundobriga were Celtic names as was Segobriga (note Gaulish *sego* 'victory', cf. German *sieg* and Celtic *briga* 'fortress').[18]

Place names in *-briga* given to fortified towns and those in *-dunum* appear to represent distinct waves of Celts onto the peninsula. The first and perhaps the older came to predominate in the western regions, e.g.,

Arabriga (near Lisbon)	Ardobrica (Galicia)
Conimbriga (near Condeixa)	Deobrigula (near Burgos)
Flaviobriga (near Bilbao)	Lacobriga (north of Palencia)
Merobriga (Algarve)	Microbriga (west of Salamanca)
Nemetobriga (Leon)	Nertobriga (Andalucía)
Talabriga (Aveiro region)	Caetobriga (Setubal)
	Volobriga (western Portugal)

From the Celtic name of the yew tree *eburo,* several place names were formed such as Eburobriga, Ebura in Andalucía, Ebora in Galicia and Evora in Portugal.[19]

Names in *dunum* are not so plentiful as those in *-briga,* the most important grouping being situated in the northeast of the peninsula, cf. Berdún (Aragón), Mavardún (in Aragón), and Verdú and Besalú in Catalonia.

A line running roughly from Huelva in the south of Spain through the vicinity of Zaragoza and northward to about San Sebastian delineates the Celtic regions of Spain as opposed to the Iberian domains on the Mediterranean side with typical toponyms in *il-.*

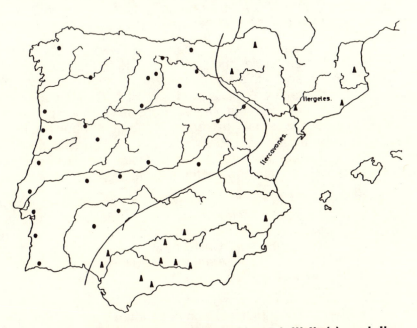

**Map 11.   Toponyms in Briga (.) and Ili-Ile(r)-and Ilu-
After Untermann (1984b)**

Celtic place names are manifest in many forms: the river Deva in Guipúzcoa, corresponding to Latin *divus* from **deivos,* appears to have been a Celtic word and Indo-European toponyms are evident in Toletum (Toledo), Vallistolitum (Valladolid), Tojos, Tollos and others that in ancient Gaul were employed to indicate 'place of the waters'.

The divinity *Bormanus (Borvo, Bormo)* 'boiling,' god of thermal springs, whose name appears in several French spa towns, contains a root *borm* found in all Celtic regions. In Spain and Portugal one finds

Bormate in Albacete, Bormella in the region of Tras-Os-Montes, and Bormoyo in Coruña, among others.

Certain toponyms in Spain and Portugal appear to have been non Celtic and yet are widespread throughout Indo-European speaking regions. Some scholars see two groups among the Indo-Europeans who infiltrated the Iberian peninsula, ushering in the Hispanic Iron Age: Those that preserved the sound /p/ in lexical items, generally place names, and those that did not. The former have been referred to as preCeltic or paraCeltic, i.e., tribes whose affiliations with Celtic are not clear but who seem to have had close linguistic relationships. The latter (those who lost the sound /p/) were Celts.20 Whether they arrived in Spain one before the other, or more or less simultaneously such as later occurred with the Visigoths, Vandals, Swabians and Alans, is not clear. In the opinion of some, the /p/-preserving groups arrived first, making them the earliest Indo-European speakers on the peninsula.

The Indo-European /p/ was preserved in Galicia in the word *pala* 'cave' reconstructed as **palla* and corresponding to Irish *all* 'stone, cliff' from Celtic **allo-*, and this from an earlier Indo-European **pallo-* /**palso-*.21 Compare Greek *pélla* and Old High German *felis* 'rock.' Also, seemingly preCeltic but Indo-European are words such as *paramus,* modern Spanish *páramo,* and the toponym Palantia (Palencia) and the tribal name Pelendones.22 A Latin inscription from Lugo in the north-west was dedicated to Poemana, a name almost identical to that of Poemani, a god of the ancient Belgians.

The diffusion of the suffix /-nt/ in Spain and Portugal may also correspond to the spread of the earliest Indo-European migrations into southwest Europe. The suffix is found in the names of rivers, e.g., Palantia (today the Mijares, near Castellón), the Arganza from **Argantia* in Asturias, the Alenza from **Alentia* in Galicia, the Arlanza and Aranzuela in the province of Burgos. (Note that /ti/ became /z/ and later /θ/ in Modern Spanish.)

While the study of Celtiberian inscriptions and coin legends indicates the general eastern boundaries of the Celtiberians, their western limits remain obscure as preRoman writing fades away in this direction. The central meseta, however, appears to have been substantially Celtic as indicated by Graeco-Latin authors and by toponyms. Most of our current perceptions concerning the names and distribution of ancient peninsular tribes stem from classical sources. Little is known of the geographical frontiers between tribes and nothing suggests that they were stable. It seems reasonable to suppose that they expanded and contracted their territories at different times in relation to the inimical behavior -- or lack of it -- of neighboring tribes.

As a large part of the classical accounts that have survived dealt with bellicose events, we are better informed about those groups that participated in the various wars with the Romans than with the tribes who remained *hors de combat.* Baetica in the south was conquered early on by the Roman legions and there seems to have been little said about the inhabitants. The Celtiberians, on the other hand, staunchly resisted Roman domination of the meseta and are widely mentioned in the historical records.

Around the time of the Roman conquest, a large part of the western meseta was occupied by the Vettones whose domains extended from near Avila to about the current border with Portugal. This territory formed the nucleus of what has been termed the culture of the Verracos. Roughly sculptured figures of animals from this area (bears, boars, pigs and bulls) seem to be related to various cults and are similar to those found further to the north.

The Vacceos occupied the central zone of the Duero plains, an area that corresponds today to the provinces of Palencia and Valladolid between the Cantabrian mountains to the north, and the Guadarrama to the south. They appear to have been more occupied with agriculture than were their neighbors and, according to a text by Diodorus, to have had a peculiar political system involving "agrarian collectivization" in which the land was divided by lot each year, and each family worked the patch of land they had acquired by chance. At the end of the season, the harvest was pooled and allotted to each family according to its needs.

The central and southern portion of the meseta was shared by the Carpetanos and Oretanos. Both occupied extensive areas but information is sketchy. The Carpetanos were a pastoral people, not greatly different from the Vettones. Accordingly to Ptolomy, they settled around Complutum, now the city of Alcalá de Henares, and Toletum (Toledo), and extended into La Mancha.

The Oretanos were established in the upper regions of the river Guadalquivir. Theirs were the towns of Castula (Cazlona) in the province of Jaén, Sisapo now Almadén, and Mirobriga in the region of Badajoz. Their southern boundaries reached into Andalucía and the northern frontier stretched onto the meseta. Classical sources place the Oretanos in the European camp but much of their territory has yielded Iberian or Iberian-Tartessian remains. Their ethnic and linguistic affiliations remain obscure.

The widespread presence of Celts on the peninsula from the Pyrenees to the Atlantic coasts is clear from statements of classical authors and archaeological details, but their linguistic similarities and divergences may never be recaptured in any substantial form, The documentation that exists for Celtiberian, however, does help establish its position among Indo-European languages in general, and among

Celtic languages in particular. The phonological make-up of Hispano-Celtic, as revealed by the documentation, also points the way to a more specific determination of substratum influences that helped shape peninsular Romance languages during the period of Roman hegemony.

In the west and northwest of the peninsula, writing was later and learned from the Romans. The inscriptional material is less plentiful, in Roman script and well influenced by Latin. A Lusitanian inscription *Lamas de Moledo* opens with the lines:

RVFIN ET TIRO SCRIPSERVNT
VEAMNICORI DOENTI ANVCOM

The text begins with the message that it was written by Rufinus and Tiro. The word *veamnicori* appears to have been a proper name but the form *doenti* seems to be a verb with Indo-European primary endings in third person plural active, and clearly related to an early *donti* as found, for example, in Greek *didonti*, but with the reduplication.23

Indo-European characteristics of the Lusitanian documentation are also evident from other grammatical properties, for example, the suffix *-ko*, or its sonorized form *-go*, of Indo-European provenance, is common.

Inscriptions from the north of Spain (Galicia and Asturias) clearly link this region with Hispano-Indo-European communities but linguistic affiliations have been uncertain. Recently, however, inscriptional material of the northern areas has come under close scrutiny with the results suggesting (albeit somewhat indirectly) that Lusitanian and Galician-Asturian formed a fairly homogeneous linguistic group displaying closely affiliated inscriptions.

Indigenous divine names in Portugal and Galicia frequently revolve around the gods or goddesses *Bandu, Bandi, Cossu, Nabia* and *Reve*.24 For example,

Bandei Brialeacui	(Beira Baixa)
Coso Udaviniago	(La Coruña)
Cosiovi Ascanno	(Asturias)
deo domeno Cusu Neneoeco	(Douro Littoral)
Reo Paramaeco	(Lugo)
Reve Laraucu	(Orense)
Reve Langanidaeigui	(Beira Baixa)25

In both Portugal and Galicia, the local theolatry was exchanged after romanization by general terms such as *deus, dominus, Lar* and *Nympha* for *Bandu, Bandi, Cossu, Nabia* and *Reve* (but not for specific Roman gods), suggesting the earlier forms were general concepts for deities.

Only in a few inscriptions were specific Roman gods mentioned:

Iove Ladico (i.e., Jupiter)	(Orense)
Marti Cariocieco	(Ponte Vedra)
dea Ataecina Turibrig(ensis) Proserpina	(Mérida)

While the Lusitanian-Galician regions seem to have been unified culturally and, it appears from the commonality of names and structures, linguistically, some dialectal differences seem to have occurred although no isoglosses can be determined. Inscriptional sources do indicate variation, such as

Aranco Aranio	(Estremadura and Cascais)
Arantio Tanginiciaeco	(Beira Baixa)
Arentiao Cronisensi	(Beira Baixa)

Similarly, two inscriptions from Beira Alta contain

Bandi Oilienaeco
Coso Oenaeco

that is, [oili-] and [oi-] plus [aiko].

Inscriptions in both areas suggest that lenition was in progress but still in free variation, cf.

Reve Langanidaeigui [-d-]	(Beira Baixa)
(Re)ve Langanitaeco [-t-]	(Beira Baixa)

While it appears that the western peninsular societies and languages were fairly uniform, does this uniformity extend to the Celtiberian regions? Here, opinions differ.

To the east of a north-south line running from Mérida to Oviedo the inscriptional material contains few references to deities and refers nearly exclusively to persons -- often in a well-known formula with the name of an individual being given, the name of the person's father in the genitive case and the indication of the clan derived by the suffix *-iko* or *-oko*, placed in the genitive plural. For example, *Arco Ambati f. Carmalicum*

93

where *Ambati* derived from *Ambatus* and *Carmalicum* from *Camalus* reads: "*Arco,* son of *Ambatus* of the *Camalus* clan."26

To the west of this line, the inscriptional documentation, much of it in the form of votive offerings, refers in large degree to the names of indigenous deities.

Besides a clear dissimilitude between east and west in the socio-religious orientation of the peninsular Indo-European inhabitants, phonological, morphological and lexical differences also stand out. The first line on a Lusitanian inscription from Cabeço das Fraguas attests to these divergencies:

Oilam Trebopala

Indi Porcom Laebo

While the language of the document is clearly of Indo-European origin, it differs from Celtiberian in vocabulary such as the name of the god *Laebo* in the dative singular, morphologically with the use of the coordinating conjunction *indi* whereas Celtiberian employed *-cue,* an enclitic, and phonologically in the preservation of *p-* as in the word *porcom* 'pig,' lost in Celtiberian.

These linguistic factors and the cultural differences evident in the two regions of the peninsula have fostered the view that the populations of the western areas spoke a non Celtic language of Indo-European origin, related perhaps to Ligurian or some other ill-defined preCeltic or Proto-Celtic group who migrated on to the Hispanic stage sometime before the Celts.27

Those who espouse the view of two different Indo-European languages spoken in Spain and Portugal in preRoman times attribute the similarities between them to borrowings. There is good reason, however, to assume that the Indo-European regions of the peninsula, during this early period, were simply Celtic-speaking albeit with important dialectal variations. The linguistic differences between the western and eastern peninsular Indo-European languages must be weighted against the similarities and conclusions drawn. Across what appears to have been rather different socio-religious practices in the two areas, many common linguistic features occur.

Onomastic studies point the way to a number of similarities between eastern and western Indo-European Hispanic languages. Some toponyms, especially those ending in *-briga,* cf. *Nemetobriga* (Galicia), *Conimbriga* (central Portugal), *Nertobriga, Arcobriga, Segobriga,* etc. in Celtiberian territory clearly link up the two areas although the form could have been borrowed. Similarly, the root *Seg-* in place names, as in *Segobriga* and *Segontius,* found in Celtiberian areas, also occurred in Asturias and in the eastern portion of Lusitania.[28] In other words, *Sego-* predominated in Celtiberia but was not lacking in Asturias.[29]

Among anthroponyms, the name *Ambatus/-a* was employed in east and west, i.e., in Lusitania and in the north of Celtiberia. *Boutius* is found principally in central Lusitania but also in Galicia and Celtiberian areas.

The Lusitanian-Galician name *Cossu* appears to have a counterpart in *Cossouci* on an inscription from Sigüenza in Celtiberian territory.

Similarities in morphological features are also in evidence: in the Lusitanian-Galician areas divine names often were accompanied by epithets which were in turn marked by suffixes, the most common having been *-ko* and *-ka* or their sonorized variants, cf. *oenaeco, daviniago, viliaego.* The same Indo-European suffix is well attested in Celtiberian documents as, for example, *neseltuco* and *areko.* [30] The word *pusinca* is found both in Galicia and the Ebro regions.[31]

The ending employed in the name *Bandue* is reminiscent of the Celtiberian word *Luguei* that contains the Indo-European ending *-ei* for thematic stems in *-u.* The plural forms *Lucubo(s)* and *Lucoub(os)* on Galician inscriptions are similar to the somewhat latinized Celtiberian word *Lugovibus* on a document from Uxama.

Some aspects of Lusitanian-Galician relate to an even larger Celtic geographical sphere than the Iberian peninsula further nudging the language of western Iberia into the Celtic camp.

The goddess *Lahe* (dative form) is attested twice in the department of the Haute Garonne and compares favorably with the Lusitanian-Galician *Lahus* as in

Laho Paraliomega   (Lugo)

The god or goddess *Ilurbeda* (Salamanca) was also venerated in areas of ancient Lusitania, as in

Ilurbedae   (Beira Littoral)

and presents an interesting comparison with *Illurberixus Anerexo* and *deo Iluroni* found in votive inscriptions of the Basque-Aquitanian region. The word *Anderoni* on a document now lost has also been reported from Galicia.

The divine name *Lucubo(s)* also occurs outside the peninsula again in the plural, in Celtic Helvetia where in the nominative form it is *Lugoves.*[32] *Lug* was also an Irish god who was said to possess all the superior qualities of the tribe. The Milky Way was known as Lug's Chain. The ancient name of Lyon was *Lugdunum (Lug dunum* and may also bear a connection with the Lusitanian-Galician name.

Some inscriptions show only the accompanying or qualifying complements of adjectives without the name of the deity:

Parameco	(Asturias)
Tabudico	(Beira Littoral)
Turiaco	(Douro Littoral)
Bormanico	(Minho)

The Lusitanian words *Bormanicus* and *Bormanus-Bormana,* attested in Celtic votive inscriptions of ancient Gaul, bear close resemblance. The former is from the thermal station of Caldas de Vizela of the Minho area, while the Gaulish names were once venerated at Aix-en-Provence and Aix-en-Diois, both hot spring sites.[33] The word comes from the Indo-European adjective *g^whormo-* which gave rise to Old Latin *formus,* Greek *thermos* and English *warm.*

The form *Cand-* which occurs in invocations such as *Candeberonio,* (Minho), *Candamo* and Latinized *Candamus* (Asturias), is reminiscent of *Cant-* current in toponyms and anthroponyms on the peninsula and in Celtic Gaul.[34]

The names *Camalus* and *Camala* are concentrated in Galicia and northern Portugal, while *Camul-* occurs in personal and divine names in Gaul and Britain as well as in local and ethnic names in Gaul, Spain, Britain and Galatia. The most likely insular Celtic cognate seems to be Irish *cam* 'battle, conflict,' if the three words *camul-, camal-* and *cam* are related.[35]

Lusitanian-Galician *toudo,* mentioned below, also has its counterpart in the well known Gaulish word *teutates.* The words *crougin* and *crougeai* on the inscription from Lamas de Moledo in Portugal compare favorably with Irish *cruach* 'heap, throng' and *nimidi* which seems to be a local variant of Gaulish *nemeton* 'holy woods' is undoubtedly related to Irish *nemed* 'sanctuary.' One inscription, for example, reads:

nimidi fiduenarum   (Douro Littoral)

In which *fiduenarum* suffixed with a Latin genitive plural morpheme, appears derived from a word that coincides with Irish *fid* 'wood.' The notion that the inscription has something to do with a sanctuary of the gods of the forest seems reasonable.[36]

Returning to the inscription from Cabeço das Fraguas (engraved on stone in the second century, A.D.), seemingly a sacrificial document, much of the vocabulary can be related to Celtic in a broad context:

> *oilam:* Old Irish *oi* 'ewe,' Gallic *ewig,* Cornish *euhic* 'doe' from Proto-Indo-European **owi.* [37]

> *trebopala:* Old Irish *treb* 'house,' Welsh *tref* 'homestead,' from Old Welsh *treb* ' dwelling, Gallic village'. The form *treb* also occurs in *trebarne* and *trebaron* in western documents and is seemingly the same word found in the Celtiberian place name (town) *Contrebia,* the river *Trebia* in northern Italy, the *Atrebares* in Gaul.

> *indi:* while clearly not related to Celtiberian *-cue,* the word does resemble Gallic *etic* 'and.'

> *porcom:* the accusative of **porkos,* Old Irish *orc.*

> *Laebo:* name of a divinity.

Parallel to *trebopala,* Lusitanian inscriptions record *toudopala* (Caceres)[38] from **teuta* 'people, nation,' which gave rise to Irish *tuath,* the divine names *Teutates* from Gaul and *Toutiorix* from the Danubian regions.

While chronology, migrations and diffusion of Hispanic Indo-European peoples are still far from clear, there is justification for assuming that there was a Celtic dialect of ancient Portugal and northwest Spain. Linguistic similarities between these western peninsular Indo-Europeans, Celtiberians, Gauls and the Celtic peoples of Great Britain are attested by affiliations in vocabulary and linguistic structure.

FOOTNOTES

1For this inscription from Peñalba de Villaster, see Lejeune 1955, p. 29, and Tovar 1961, p. 80, who have recorded it as *Turos*

Carorum.uiros.ueramos. The above rendering is from Faust 1975, p. 197. Tovar translates the line as "Tutus Carorum uir supremus."

[2]The latin term *Celtiberian* seems to refer to an alliance of indigenous Celtic tribes banded together against the Roman threat, but the designation remains unclear in relation to ethnic mixture and geographical extension. For some detail on this question, see Schmoll 1959, Koch, 1979 and Untermann l984b.

[3]The Arevacos may have been a western branch of the Vacceos. The area of the headwaters of the Duero was fairly well peopled in preRoman fimes. Tiberius Sempronius Gracchus claimed to have conquered three hundred cities in Celtiberia Citerior -- this was no doubt an exaggeration -- the remains of fifty-four native towns only have survived. See Livermore. The population of Celtiberia as defined above has been estimated at about 340,000. The city of Numantia (Soria) contained about 8,000 inhabitants, Termantia about 6,500, Segeda about 5,000, etc.

[4]Tovar, *op cit.,* p. 77.

[5]The Olcades, Lobetanos and Turboletas were mentioned in classical sources but of imprecise geographical location.

[6]Among the Celtiberians the bull constituted an important feature of sacred belief as seems to have been the case with the Iberians. Celtiberian tesserae of hospitality and of a religious nature were inscribed on bronze which often took the form of this animal.

[7]Forms collected first by Pokorny and augmented by Lapesa, Tovar, Schmoll, *et al.*

[8]See Tovar, *op. cit.,* p. 79.

[9]The consonantal system was presented first by Lejeune. The phonological status of [s] and [r] conforming to the use of the Iberian signs is not clear.

[10]See Tovar, *op. cit.* and *ELH* Vol. I, p. 104. For the Gaulish form see Whatmough, 1970, p. 972.

[11]Tovar, *op. cit.,* p. 81.

[12]Lewis and Pedersen, pp. 26-7. For other possibilities of phonological change in Celtiberian (lenition, loss of -*s,* syncope, etc.), see Tovar *op cit.*

13See Tovar 1973, Schmoll 1959 and Schwerteck, among others, for analysis of Celtiberian.

14See Tovar, *op. cit.* and Schwerteck, p. 193. The lines "to . . . comeimu" have been read by Schwerteck as 'dem Lug empfehlen wir das Ackerland' where the verbal root *mei* has a meaning something like 'mild' or 'friendliness.'

15*sistat* has been given the meaning 'consecrate' or 'sanctify.'

16See also Tovar, 1961, p. 84 and for the transliteration given here, Faust 1975.

17Some sequences in the text are obscure and have led to divergent interpretations. In other cases, while legible, the individual words have given rise to disparities in meaning. *Tocoitos,* for example, has been considered by some a tribe and a god; *litom* has been compared with Irish *laithe* and Gaulish *lat* and assigned the meaning 'day,' but some, e.g., Hoz, Michelena, considered it to have been a verb. A reading of the inscription by Maluquer de Motes, 1974, interpreted the sign generally taken to represent /r/ as /qu/. For a comprehensive study of this document see Fleuriot. The text translates roughly as follows:

'Arrangement of the convallidations of land: confirmations of sworn oaths and imposed obligation, thus: it is inauspicious that Sosaucos demolish or break or destroy the enclosing wall. He (Sosaucos?) acquires the enclosed space, setting apart in advance (deducting in advance) by the size of the property, the size of the payment of money in order to raise livestock of 100 young animals, according to the sworn oaths of properties. A boundary road will encompass a cow stable established in a circle, an enclosed field and an enclosure of stone that can be the strong defence spot up to six feet in height. That which is destined for construction are the spaces outside the boundary ditch but inside the good land extending toward the canton of irrigated? land. They will build some sheep folds (or they will sow?) for (Sosaucos?) and the boundary roads (or some furrows?) decided by himself. They will fashion the doors and the guard posts of the doors as many as the passages. What may be assigned in size, the gift of the tithe of the seeds in a single amount may be small or large, on the labours, in obligation imposed by the Akainoi. That they may not be bound by the sworn oath. This one (Sosaucos?) accepts the labour shared and the gift of the tenths of the sworn oath. The king of the Aletu? will always uphold (it) as the one who confirms the sworn oath, and the imposed obligation. We order, Abulu (chief? of the Ubi.'

[18]Some elusive and semantically impalpable words, seemingly of preCeltic times, further confound an already linguistically recondite period. The place name *Alaba,* now the province of Alava, for example, has no known relationship with Basque or other languages. Portuguese Aveiro seems to have come from a similar source, i.e., *Alaveiro.* The word *rita* often occurs in the western half of the province of Zamora meaning 'tierras de labor' in expressions such as Ritas Blancas, Rita la Silva, Rita del Becerro, and in other cases such as Campo Rita, La Cruz de Rito, etc. The word was, perhaps, an appellative of preIndo-European times. The name Rita for a goddess does occur in north Italic languages, cf. *Rita* and Venetic *Reitia.* See Pulgram pp. 41 ff.

The word *mulo* 'hornless' (not to be confused with Spanish *mulo* from Latin *mulus*) found in western Asturias has also been considered to be of ancient origin. It lacks correspondences in insular Celtic and in Gaul, but it is found in Slovenian and Ladin *mul* 'without horns,' in Lithuanian *mulas* and Lettish *mule* with the same meaning. This appears to be an example of a Hispanic word directly related to eastern Alpine and Baltic languages.

[19]Tovar, *op. cit.,* p. 119.

[20]The distinction between an earlier Indo-European layer (Ligurian) and later Celts in Spain was first made by Pokorny on the basis of place names.

[21]For another etymology of this word, see Corominas.

[22]See Tovar, *op. cit.,* p. 100.

[23]For this and other western Hispanic Indo-European inscriptions, see Faust 1975, Tovar 1961, p. 91 ff. Both analyze the word *doenti.*

[24]For these examples, see Untermann 1984.

[25]These and nearly all extant inscriptional material of the western area can be found in the papers by Albertos 1975 and Untermann 1980. The three relatively long inscriptions form Portugal, all clearly of Indo-European characteristics, are perhaps best examined in the paper by Faust 1975.

[26]Clan names may be somewhat latinized as, for example, *Medutticum/Medutticorum.* See Albertos 1975.

[27]For ancient Hispanic names contaianing /p-/, see Tovar 1961. Tovar

and Albertos share the view of an Indo-European non Celtic language spoken in the western Hispanic regions.

Indicative of the Celtic languages was the loss of Proto Indo-European /p-/ but its apparent preservation in place names and on inscriptions in the western areas of the peninsula (e.g., *porcom* on a document from Cabeço das Fraguas, cf. Latin *porcus* 'swine,' but Middle Irish *orc*) has suggested to Tovar an earlier, preCeltic Indo-European invasion of the peninsula.

[28]According to Untermann, 1984, p. 9.

[29]See Untermann, *op cit.,* Map no. 8.

[30]For these words, see Untermann 1975, Vol. I. pp. 83 and 265.

[31]According to Albertos 1979, p. 165.

[32]See Untermann, 1980.

[33]*Loc cit.*

[34]Welsh *cann* 'white, clear,' Old Breton *cant* 'full moon,' Welsh *cannaid* 'luminous, sun, moon' seem to be related forms. One northwest inscription reads *iovi candamio* 'Jupiter bright' ? '"luminous'? For Celtic words in Asturias, see Sevilla Rodriguez 1979.

[35]See Evans 1979.

[36]See Untermann 1984.

[37]See Buck.

[38]The entire inscription reads: *munidi eberobrigae toudopalandaigae.*

Chapter 7

THE BASQUE LANGUAGE

Basque is the only living western European language that is not of Indo-European provenance. The majority of its speakers dwell in Spain; the others in southwestern France. On the Spanish side of the Pyrenees, they occupy most of the province of Vizcaya, a small bit of Alava, all of Guipúzcoa and the northern quarter or so of Navarre. On the French side, the Department of the Basses Pyrenées is about half Basque.

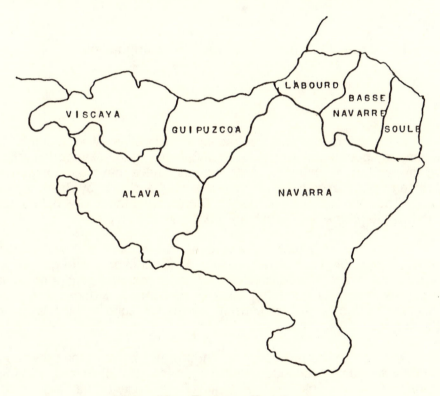

Map 12.   Basque Provinces

The number of speakers is estimated about half a million in Spain and about a fifth of that in France. Under pressure from Spanish, French, Gascon, and Catalan, the Basque language has gradually lost ground. In the Middle Ages it was spoken in most of Alava and in over half of Navarre and prior to that, Basque toponyms suggest an even more extensive distribution of speakers.

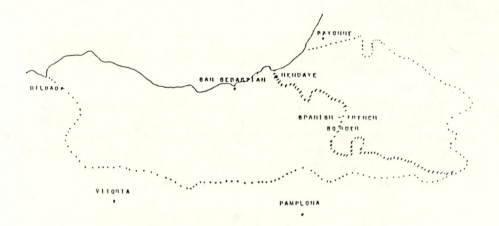

**Map 13.   Basque Linguistic Boundaries
based on Allières**

Early Basque influence has been perceived well beyond the present-day geographical limit of the language. In the Cantabrian region and the territory of Asturias, words such as *selaya* have been explained in reference to Basque [selai] 'field, meadow' and *ibio* by Basque [ibai] 'river'. The river name *Ebro* (Greek *iberus*) was taken, it would seem, from Basque [*ibara*] 'valley, estuary' (*ibar* with the article).

The views of Humboldt and even earlier scholars which were taken up by Hübner and, above all, by Schuchardt, sought in the Basques the direct descendants of the Ancient Iberians. There has been much skepticism of these opinions in the past few decades but the question of some kind of relationship between Basque and Iberian is still very much alive.[1]

The ancient name *Iliberri* for the town of Elvira in the province of Granada suggests a Basque connection in the form of *iriberri* (Basque *iri* + *berris* 'new town'). Further, Mendiculeia, a city of the llergetes and another of the same name in ancient Lusitania suggest a relationship with Basque *mendi* 'mountain'. Other names containing *mend-* were scattered throughout Spain such as *Mendoto*, *Mendoza*, *Mendones*, and *Mendello*, and in Portugal *Mendoça*, etc.[2] The name *Aspe* designating a town a little north of Elche in the province of Alicante has been compared to Basque *azpe* 'under the rock' i.e., *-pe* 'under' and *az* a variant of *aitz* 'large stone'. Toponyms that may contain a form of the suffix *-tegi* as in *Artigi* and *Astigi*, found in the southwest of the

104

peninsula have been compared to Basque *-tegi*, 'place where something is kept'.

Names similar to each other, of course, occur by chance or may be borrowed from region to region.

To the north of the present-day Basque provinces lies Aquitania in southwest France where Latin inscriptions of the first few centuries after Christ often contain personal names that appear to have been Basque.

While it is clear that toward the end of the first millennium, B.C., the Basque inhabitants of the western Pyrenees were circumscribed by Celtic populations to the west, north and south and by Iberians to the east, the geographical parameters of the ancient Basque, however, are obscure. If a few phrases in Basque from the eleventh century, A.D., recorded at the monastery of San Millán, a little south of the Ebro River in La Rioja, are indicative of the geographical extent of the language at that time, the territory of the Basque speakers has been receding steadily from then on.

The modern Basque language is strikingly different from other European languages but to capture its linguistic essence in a few statements is, of course, not possible. Some of the more salient features, however, are given here as an indication of the complexity inherent in Basque grammatical structure.

Substantives, adjectives and pronouns are declined by adding suffixes to a base form and distinguishing two types of flexions: *indeterminate* in which the noun is not specified as to number, and *determinate* which contains singular and plural and is generally characterized by a postposed article.

Nouns and adjectives employ the same suffixes throughout and descriptive adjectives follow the noun, the last receiving the suffix, cf.

etxe 'house'	*berri* 'new'
etxe berri	'new house'
etxearen	'of the house'
etxe berriaren	'of the new house'
etxe berri handiaren	'of the large new house'

The declensional system has the following characteristics:

CASE	SUFFIXES			
	Proper Names	Indefinite	Definite	
			Sing	Plural
Nominative	ø	ø	-a	-ak
Ergative	-(e)k	-(e)k	-ak	-ek
Dative	-(r)i	-(r)i	-ari	-ei
Possessive	-(r)en	-(r)en	-aren	-en
Locative	-(e)ko	-(e)tako	-(e)ko	-etako
Unitive	-(r)ekin	-(r)ekin	-arekin	-ekin
Instrumental	-(e)z	-(e)z	-az	-ez
Destinative	-(r)entzat	-(r)entzat	-arentzat	-entzat
Ablative	-(r)engatik	(r) engatik	-arengatik	-engatik
Inessive	-(r)engan	-(e)tan	-an	-etan
Elative	-(r)engandik	-(e)tatik	-(e)tik	-etatik
Allative	-(r)engana	-(e) tara	-(e)ra	-etara
Prolative	-tzat	-tzat	-	-
Partitive	-(r)ik	-(r)ik	-	-

As an ergative type language, the nominative case is used in Basque to designate the subject of an intransitive verb and the object of a transitive verb. The ergative marks the subject of a transitive verb. Compare:

Jonek Mikel ikusi du	Yon has seen Mikel
Jon kalean ibili da	Yon has walked in the street

While many of the case designations are self-explanatory, a few may require further comment.

There are two types of genitives: possessives in -*en* and possessive locatives in -*ko* marking spacial or temporal localization. The unitive translates the preposition 'with' and refers to accompaniment, while the prolative in -*tzat* marks destination and translates the preposition 'for.' The inessive in -*n* relates to position ('where' or 'to be in). '), the allative in -*ra* relates to the goal ('place where one is going, carried toward'), the elative in -*tik* marks origin ('place where one comes from, leaves from'). The partitive is equivalent to the French partitive *du*.[3]

In a manner similar to Indo-European languages, the Basque verb agrees in person and number with the subject of the sentence. Unlike these languages, however, it also agrees with the object:

Pellok etxea ikusi du	Peter has seen the house
Pellok etxeak ikusi ditu	Peter has seen the houses

The verb may be (1) intransitive or (2) transitive:

Pello joan da	Peter has gone
Pellori liburua erori zaio	The book has fallen from Peter
(Peter is dative singular)	
Pellok ikusi du	Peter has seen it
Pellok amari liburu bat erosi dio	Peter has bought a book for his mother (*bat* = 'one, a')

The verbal forms *joan, erori, ikusi, erosi* are past participles corresponding to 'gone,' 'fallen,' 'seen,' 'bought.' The words *joate, erortze, ikuste, eroste*, followed by *a* correspond to the substantive 'the going,' 'the falling,' etc. while *joaten, erortzen, ikusten, erosten* have a frequentive value. The infinitive form of these verbs is *joan, eror, ikus, eros* 'to go,' 'to fall,' etc. With the suffix -*ko* the participal form becomes *joango, eroriko, ikusiko, erosiko* and expresses future action.

The elements *da* and *du* relate information concerning personal relationships. In phrases such as *hil da* 'he died,' no agent is involved, but in *hil du* 'he killed him,' an agent is present; or *galtzen da* 'he is lost,' and *galtzen du* 'he loses it.' In general, these auxiliary forms based on *izan* 'to be,' and *ukan* 'to have' reflect the intransitive and transitive characteristics of utterances.

Between the basic verb and the auxiliary elements other components that introduce new semantic features may occur:

Nik dut	I have it (*Ni* = first person singular pronoun)
Nik jakin dut	I have known it (*jakin* = 'to know')
Nik jakin izan dut	I used to have known it
Nik jakin behar dut	I have to know it (*behar* = necessity)
Nik Jakin behar izan dut	I used to have to know it

Basque syntactic arrangements are nearly the opposite of English and the surrounding languages such as French and Spanish. Compare:

Donostia-ko alkate-aren lau etxe eder hori-ek
    1   2   3   4   5 6
Those four beautiful houses of the mayor of San Sebastian
    6   3   5   4   2   1

Zu-k esan di-zki-gu-zu
            1 2 3
You have told them to us
 3   1   2
Gu-k esan di-zki-zu-gu
          1 1 3
We have told them to you
 2   1   3

In examples (2) and (3) the verb agrees with the indirect complement.[4]

Besides participating as an auxiliary in periphrastic constructions of the type *ikusten dut* 'I see it,' a verb such as *ukan* may be employed alone in a strong capacity to render the idea of possession, i.e., *dut* 'I have it' (*d* = 'it,' *u* = 'have,' *t* = 'I').

Basque has the general features of an agglutinating type language, cf.

dut	I have it
dugu	We have it
dugun	that we have (-*n* = 'that')
duguna	that we have it
dukegu	We can have it
dukegun	that which we can have
dukeguna	that we can have it
dukegunarentzat	for that which we can have

and,

banu	*ba-* = 'if' = 'I'
	-n- = 'I'
	u = 'had it' (from *ukan* 'to have')
banitu	*-it-* = 'them' i.e., pluralizer of complement
	'If I had them.'
bazinitu	*-zin-* = 'you'
	'If you had them.'
bazinituzte	*-z-* = second pluralizer of complement
	-te = 'you all' or pluralizer of subject or
	-zte = general pluralizer
	'If you all had them'

Attempts have been made to establish the origin of the Basque people by comparing their language with the Hamitic languages of North Africa, with the Caucasian languages of the Caucasus, and with the inscriptions of the ancient Iberians. In each case the results have been inconclusive and predicated on unsubstantiated suppositions. For example, when comparing Basque and Berber (a group of languages of North Africa pertaining to the larger Hamitic family of languages) some striking similarities among vocabulary items occur:

Basque		**Berber**	
aker	'he-goat'	iker, aker	'mutton'
anai		ana	'brother'
izen		izm	'name'
zamari		zagmarz	'mare'

Similarly, some morphological features appear to be common to both. Compare the definite article in *a* employed as a suffix:

Basque		**Berber**	
gizon<u>a</u>		argaz<u>a</u>	'the man'
etxe<u>a</u>	'the house'	tamgart<u>a</u>	'the woman'

Basque comparisons with Berber, however, quickly dry up. The only conclusion that may be drawn to date is that some words are accidentally similar and a few others may have been borrowed.[5]

Some scholars adhere to the hypothesis that a Caucasian-type language was introduced into the West by migratory people from Asia Minor who arrived in southern Spain about 2000 B.C.[6]   Such a hypothesis helped explain Basque-type names in southern Spain such as *Bilbilis* which was first noted by Von Humboldt.

Vocabulary items that have been compared favorably between Basque and Caucasian appear to point to phonological correspondences in which glottalized sibilants or palatals in the Caucasian languages seem to correspond to a medio-palatalized sibilant in Basque, i.e., [ṣ] or [tṣ], and the Caucasian nonglottalized equivalents, whether voiceless or voiced, appear to correspond to the Basque sibilants [s] or [ts].   Thus, Basque *su* [ṣu] 'fire,' where [tṣ-] > [ṣ-] corresponds to Caucasian (Lago) [t'su] 'fire.'   The diacritic /'/ as in Caucasian [t'] represents glottalization.

An old plural suffix in Basque, *-tzu* [tsu], corresponds to the plural suffix [-tsᵂa] in North Caucasian Abkhaz.

Basque *zu* [su] 'you,' an old form for 'you,' plural, has its counterpart in North Caucasian [sᵂe] 'you,' plural.   The word *antz* [ants] 'toward' in Basque is equivalent to Abkhaz [(a)ndza] 'toward.'[7]

These and other concordances, according to Lafon, are not to be explained by chance nor by loan words.   He labels the language group in which he perceived both Basque and Caucasian as belonging to a Euscaro-Caucasian family of langauges.[8]

These supposed relationships in a Euscaro-Caucasian grouping have been objected to by linguists on the grounds that they are too tenuous and too few to establish a family of languages and that as several of the Caucasian languages are compared with Basque, the chances of accidental similarities are significantly raised.   These objections become more cogent when one considers that the Caucasian languages have been ill-studied, are extremely diverse, and are not yet classified satisfactorily within a Caucasian family, not to mention a larger grouping.

Similarities between Basque and Caucasian languages, including the use of the ergative case in both, do not necessarily imply a migration from the Caucasus to the Pyrenees, but could have been due to a common language of remote times whose speakers spread throughout the Mediterranean basin.

Lacking positive migratory evidence concerning the Basques, the alternative, an *in situ* development of Cro-Magnon Man, appears to be acceptable to many Basque scholars.[9]

Just as Basque names south of the Pyrenees suggest a once more-widespread distribution of Basque speakers, similarly, the region in southwest France (designated Aquitania by the Romans) appears to have been inhabited by Basques in preRoman times. The ancient Aquitanian language, known mainly from anthroponyms and toponyms, has lexical features in common with Basque

Aquitanian texts are brief, often one or two words, and consist of about four hundred personal and seventy divine names. The inscriptions were written in the Roman alphabet.

In the realm of phonology, Aquitanian like Basque seems to have lacked the sound [f], had no word initial [r], appears to have had no sound [p] and added a prothetic vowel before the word initial consonant cluster [st-].

Complicating the overall picture are Celtic names found in the toponymy, anthroponomy and among some common words of both areas.[10]

Proper names, both of mortals and divinities, from Roman inscriptions of southwest France but which are neither Latin nor Celtic are often similar or identical to Basque names. Consequently, the ancient language spoken throughout Aquitania has been considered historically as a form of Basque or a Basque-related dialect.[11] Compare:

Basque		Aquitanian
abere	'domestic animal'	Aberri deo
adin	'age'	Dannadinnis
ak(h)er	'billy-goat'	Aherbelste deo
argi	'light'	Argesis
asto	'donkey'	Asto (Ilunno)
beltz	'black'	Belex
berri	'new'	Eliberre
bihotz	'heart	Bihozus
bortz	'five'	Borso
erdi	'half, middle'	Erditse
euskara	'Basque'	Ausci
gar	'flame'	Garunna, Garre deo
gizon	'man'	Cison
gorri	'red'	Bigorra, Calagorris
herauts	'boar'	Harausoni
idi	'ox'	Idiatte deo[12]

111

hartz	'bear'	Harsus
ilun	'dark'	Iluno, Ilun(n)i deo
laur	'four'	Laurco
lur	'earth'	Lurgorr-
neska, neskato	'girl'	Nescato (in fem. names)
otso	'wolf'	Oxson
sei/seiñ	'child'	seni[13] (in masc. names)
seme	'son'	Sembetel, Sembedonis (*sembe-* in masc. names)
suri	'white'	Sirico
ur	'water'	Atur
zuzen	'right (handed)'	Sosonnis

A number of the Aquitanian names refer to gods and have Basque connections. The billy-goat, prominent in Basque tales as *ak(h)er beltz* 'black goat' can be seen in the Aquitanian divinity *Aherbelste deo.* Similarly, Aquitanian *Marti Arixoni* seems to exhibit the Basque word *aritz* 'oak.' Basque *neskato* 'girl' appears on Roman inscriptions of the region, and *Cison,* derived no doubt from Basque *gizon,* was a proper name.

The Basque word *seme* could be of Indo-European origin, *sen- + suffix *-be* giving Aquitanian *sembe-* and Basque [mb > m] *seme.* Compare Old Irish *sen* 'old.' The suffix *-be* could be related to Basque -*pe/be* 'below.'

Similarities between Aquitanian and Iberian also occur primarily among proper names in Aquitania and theose found for the most part on the Ascoli Bronze:

Aquitanian	**Iberian**
Dannadinnis	Adingibas, Ilduradin, etc.
Baeserte deo	Belasbaiser, . . .nespaiser
Belendi	Belennes
-beles	Umarbeles
Bihox-	Biosildun (Alcoy II)
Ennebox	Enneges
Ilun(n)i deo	Nereildun
Seniponnis (possibly Celtic)	Sanibelser
Sosonnis	Sosimilus, Sosinbiuro

Ta<u>ls</u>conis	Tautin<u>dals</u>
Semb<u>etel</u>	Biurt<u>etel</u>
Tor<u>s</u>teginno	Tor<u>s</u>inno

If Iberian shows similarities to Aquitanian and the latter was a dialect of Basque, then one should expect to find similarities between Iberian and Basque. Many such forms are, in fact, in evidence but how best to account for them is another matter.

FOOTNOTES

[1]Von Humbolt in 1821 considered Basque to have been the last vestige of the Iberian language and Schuchardt in 1909 tried to establish a grammatical connection between Iberian and Basque through a comparison of their declensional systems, a study not accepted today. For more recent views of a positive nature on Iberian-Basque connections see Verd, Oroz, Pattison and Beltrán Villagrasa.

[2]*mendi* may not, of course, have been an original or native Basque word, cf. Latin *mōns, montis*, Celtic (Breton) *menez*, Welsh *mynydd*. Celtic words survive in Basque to the present day such as *mando* 'mule' corresponding to the Latin borrowing from Celtic *mannus* 'a small Gallic pony.' The word may appear in the name of the Hispano-Celtic chief *Mandonius.*

[3]Nouns ending in a consonant add a vowel if the suffix is consonantal, e.g., Nom. *Martin,* Erg. *Martinek,* but cf. *Haltsu, Haltsuk.* If the noun ends in a vowel and the suffix begins with a vowel, an /r/ is inserted, e.g., poss. gen. *Haltsuren,* dat. *Haltsuri,* etc.

[4]See Urkizu, pp. 23,25 for these examples. For a comprehensive treatment of the Basque verb, see Lafitte.

[5]For examples, see Mukarovsky.

[6]For a treatment of the subject, see Bouda.

[7]Lafon 1960 p. 94.

[8]For a phonological perspective on several Caucasian languages, see Ruhlen.

[9]In the view of some investigators interested in the risky business of linguistic paleontology, lexical items appear to preserve forms from the Stone Age. Of interest in this connection is the word *hortzi* [hortsi] 'lightning' which incorporates the word *hortz* [horts] 'tooth.' In European prehistoric times, a tooth carried on a necklace constituted protection against lightning. The word *lur* 'earth, ground,' appears to contain the same root as *elur* 'snow,' suggesting that it dates back to the period of widespread glaciation. Similarly, the Basque word for stone *arri* or *harri,* and that for ice, *karro,* appear related. The lexical item *orma* which refers to a wall, e.g., of rock or a partition wall, in Biscay, has also the meaning of 'ice' in Navarre, Labourd and Guipúzcoa, etc. See Charpentier.

[10]The word *andere* 'woman' for example, common to Basque and Aquitanian, appears borrowed from Celtic, cf. Middle Irish *ainder* 'young woman.'

[11]Luchaire believed this to be the case as early as 1877. Note the name *Vascones* which gave rise to the designation *Basques* (but *Euskara* in the language) also seems to have been the origin of the name Gascones.

[12]See also Schwartz who analyzes *Idiatte deo* as *Idi* 'ox' plus -*a* a postposed article and -*tte* a collective suffix.

[13]For these words and other variants in Basque, see Michelena 1977, p. 302.

Chapter 8

ANCIENT IBERIAN RELATIONSHIPS

It is generally known that the Basque language of the northeastern Hispanic peninsula and the southwestern corner of France has no substantiated antecedents. Similarly, ancient Iberian, a preRoman language of Mediterranean Spain and southern France, perceived only through inscriptional material (still undeciphered and in some aspects problematical) also has no identifiable progenitors.

Basque and Iberian existed in adjacent and perhaps overlapping areas of the Hispanic peninsula, however, and a kind of linguistic imbrication is supposed to account for the personal names and other forms common to both languages. For example, inscribed on the Ascoli Bronze Tablet[1] are personal names from locations thought to have been situated north of the Ebro River (Aragón), where the commissure of the two cultures and languages would be most expected. Compare for instance the following:

Basque		**Iberian**
adin	'age'	Adin
biur	'twisted'	Biur-
beltz [belts]	'black, dark'	Bels/Beles
zuzen [susen]	'right, fair'	Sosin-

It is clear from these and other forms on the Ascoli Bronze that the names were not simply Basque as they are found elsewhere on Iberian inscriptions, for example:

Adinbelaur	(Tarragona)
Biuru	(Castellón)
Ikorbeles	(Sagunto)
Sosinbiuru	(Castellón)

Similarities between Ancient Iberian and Basque are numerous and provocative. In spite of this, some investigators reject any putative relationship of the two languages beyond simple borrowing on the basis that Basque has not proven to be the key to unlock the semantic secrets of Iberian inscriptions.

Apparent similarities between ancient Iberian and modern Basque have prompted several points of view regarding their relationship:

Basque has been seen as a living continuation of Iberian, or a direct descendant; the two have been seen as dialects of a common ancestor with Iberian dying out; both Basque and Iberian were influenced by a common substratum language but were not themselves related.[2] Another perspective is simply that Basque and Iberian were distinct languages mutually influenced by borrowings.[3]

While the once-prevailing idea that Basque was a direct descendant of Iberian has largely evaporated, other considerations concerning their relationship have become more prominent. What is there about the two languages that has prompted so much learned exchange and discussion? There are conflicting views, several possibilities, but so far, little in the way of unambiguous facts on which to make categorical claims. The Iberian-Basque similarities in linguistic structure that are perhaps most evident are outlined in the following pages.

A composite schematic representation of the Basque phonological system presents the following characteristics:

		CONSONANTS				
		labial	dental	prepalatal	palatal	velar
Occlusives	voiceless	p	t		t^y	k
	voiced	b	d		y	g
Fricatives		(f)	s	ṣ	š	
Affricates			ts	tṣ	tš	
Nasals		m	n		ñ	
Lateral			l		λ	
Vibrants	flap		r			
	trill		ṛ			

VOWELS				DIPHTHONGS
	front		back	
High	i		u	ei
				ai
Mid		e	o	oi
				eu
Low		a		au

116

Along with voiceless and voiced occlusives, Basque contains a voiceless sibilant /s/ (written as z), a medio-palatalized or retroflex voiceless sibilant /ṣ/ (written as s), and a voiceless palatal /š/ (written as x). Opposed to these fricatives is a series of affricates /ts/, /tṣ/ and /tš/ (written tz, ts, and tx, respectively). A voiceless labial-dental fricative /f/ occurs in some dialects[4] but generally not in native words.

The consonants /t, d, l, n/ may have palatalized counterparts (written as tt, j, ll and ñ). The vibrants /r/ and /rr/ (the latter transcribed here as [ṛ]) comprise two distinct phonemes, e.g., /bero/ 'hot,' and /beṛo/ 'an animal resembling a wild boar.'

Any statements about the two languages are necessarily hampered by the fact that on the one hand the Iberian syllabary disguises in large measure the true underlying phonological nature of the language, and on the other hand, nothing definitely is known about the Basque language twenty-five centuries ago. There are no written records exclusively and unambiguously Basque earlier than the Late Middle Ages. While the absence of documentation may deny a precise analysis of the relationship between Basque and Iberian, and for that matter, Aquitanian, the mutual linguistic influence they had on each other (perhaps not unlike that of Basque and Spanish) is nevertheless quite evident.

Basque and Iberian Phonology

The palatal order of sounds in Basque appears to have consisted of variants of the non palatal phonemes in ancient times. The ancient language also seems to have lacked [p] and [m], sounds that developed later through modifications such as [nb] > [mb] > [m] and from borrowings. Ancient Basque seems to have had a phonological structure approximating the following:[5]

[ ]	t	ts	tṣ	k
b	d			g
[ ]		s	ṣ	
[ ]	n			
	l			
	r			
	ṛ			

117

The reconstructed Basque phonological system is strikingly similar to ancient Iberian, judging from inscriptional material, leading to the suspicion that Iberian [ṣ] and [s] (written M and ⟨) may have paralleled Basque [ṣ] and [s][6] (or [tṣ] and [ts]). The fact that Basque [ṣ] and [s] etc., have merged in some Basque dialects lends some credence to the possibility that these were common to both Iberian and Basque and may also have merged in Iberian. Compare the Iberian phonological system as constructed from orthographic forms. Note the presence of only one labial sound in both languages or, conversely, the absence of [p], [m] and [f] and the occurrence of two *r*- type sounds.

[ ]	t			k
b	d			g
[ ]		s	ṣ	
[ ]	n			
	l			
	r			
	ṛ			

Both Basque and ancient Iberian seem to have had close parallels between their respective vocalic systems, each containing five vowels based on the place of articulation of front and back and three degrees of aperture.

Basque vowels have remained conservative, cf.

Basque			**Aquitanian**	
seme	'child'		sembe-	
nesakto	'girl'		nescato	[neskato]
bi(h)ots	'heart'		bihox-	[bihoṣ-]
gison	'man'		cison	[kison]
il(h)un	'dark'		ilun	

The five vowel system of Basque

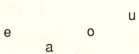

i   u
e   o
a

compares favourably with the postulated five vowel system of ancient Iberian:

i   u

e   o

a

Basque consonants may all occur in word initial position with the exception of [r-]. This also seems to be the case in Iberian. Any consonant in Basque, with the exception of voiced occlusives [b, d, g] is permitted to occur in word final position. Again, Iberian appears to have had about the same distributional arrangement although, unlike Basque, a word final [-g] appears in the written documentation of the Greek alphabetic scripts, but it may have been an abbreviation in this position. The most frequent consonants in word final position in both Basque and Iberian are [-n], [-r], and [-s] (or Basque [ts]), much less often [-1]. The occlusives [-t] and [-k] are of relatively rare occurrence in Basque, confined primarily to the declensional system. Their occurrence in Iberian and Aquitanian also appears to have been infrequent but found, for example, on the Alcoy Lead Tablet, cf. *bagarok, gaibigait* and in Aquitanian *Hannac Andossic.*[7]

Iberian had no orthographic sign for the sound [p], a sound that probably did not exist in a contrastive function but may have occurred as a variant of [b]. The sound [p] occurs several times on the Ascoli Bronze Tablet written in Roman script, cf. *Estopeles* and *Luspannar.* Similarly, Old Basque seems to have had no contrastive [p] but, as indicated on Aquitanian inscriptions it may have occurred as a variant of [b] in *Andoxponni* (dative case) and *Senniponis* (genitive case) where *pon* was written instead of the more normal *bon* suggesting some free variation of the two sounds.

Distributional Features of Basque

Consonant and consonant combinations in Basque display a good deal of common ground in their distributional arrangements with Iberian. Both reject certain combinations such as an occlusive + occlusive, e.g., [bd], [dk], and [bk] or [gb] and occlusive + non-occlusive sequences [bs], [bn?], [bl], [br], [tr]. [tl], [ks], [kl], [kr], etc. Latin loan words incorporated into Old Basque indicate that this situation existed in early times. Either a vowel was inserted to break up the consonant cluster, cf.

Latin	Basque
astru	asturu
fronte	boronte
libru	liburu
lucru	lukuru

or one of the consonants disappeared both in borrowed words, e.g., Latin *piuma* > Basque *luma*, and in Basque compounds:

bait	+nais	>	bainais
*oroit	+ men	>	oroipen[8]

In accordance with Iberian renderings of foreign words, a name such as that of the deity *Proteus* would have appeared in Iberian as *borote* plus an Iberian ending, e.g., -*n*.[9] The word *boroten* occurred as a name in the inscription *borotenbotenin* [10] in which, as commonly happened in Iberian, one name was partially repeated in the other:

boroten
bo ten in

Again, judging from Latin loans, early Basque avoided word initial consonant clusters, along with Iberian, as far as one can determine from the documentation:

Latin	**Basque**
placet	laket
clarus	laru
gloria	loria[11]

Both languages, on the other hand, support medial combinations of the type non-occlusive + occlusive, e.g., [-st-], [-rk-], [-nd-], [-ld-], etc.

Modern Basque dialects also show phonological alternations between [m], [mb] and [nb], cf.

linbur		anbil	
	'slipping'		'precipitate'[12]
limbur		amil	

Again, borrowings manifest the reduction of this combination of consonants:

Latin	**Basque**
ambitionem	amisione

Spanish	
convento [kombento]	komentu
convenio [kombenio]	komenio

The ancient language of Aquitania exhibits [mb], cf. *sembe-*, which continues in Basque *seme* 'son.' A parallel change is seen in Iberian where [nb] > [m] (cf. the Ascoli Bronze). Basque contains the sequences *ildu* 'cultivated field,' *illun* 'darkness' or *ilun* where [ld] appears to have become in some cases [ll] or [l]. In this respect there is a parallel with Iberian and Aquitanian,

	Iberian	[ld, ll, l]
[ld]	Basque	[ld, ll, l]
	Aquitanian	[l]

The assimilation to [ll] and [l] did not spread to all words except, perhaps, in Aquitanian, cf. *Illuni deo.*

Names seemingly borrowed into Latin and Greek suggest that the assimilations were occurring during Classical times, cf. Iberian *ilduro* on coins and Latin *Iluro,* today, Mataró.

Examples of [l] in Iberian appear to correspond to earlier [ld] as in *ilurtibas* (Vall d'Uxo) that may be reconstructed as **ildurtibas..* Compare also the name *Illurtibas* on the Ascoli Bronze, but *ildu-* on the Alcoy Lead Tablet and *Ilduradin.*[13]

Syncope seems to have occurred in Iberian, Aquitanian and perhaps Basque dating back to the Iberian period and in similar positions in the compound word compare:

Iberian	beles/bels	bels	(Bennabels)
Basque		belts	
Aquitanian	belex [beleş]	bels	(aherbelste deo)

Judging from *Adimels (Adin-beles), Atabels, Anbels, Bennabels,* as opposed to *Beles* syncope occurred in Iberian when *Beles* was the second (and unstressed?) member of a compound.

Modern Basque dialects show a similar situation: [erets] becomes [erts] 'edge, border' (that is, it undergoes syncope) in compounds such as [itsaserts] 'edge of the sea.'

Some words that appear to have been common to both Basque and Iberian and which evince syncope in Basque are:

Iberian	Basque	
alatesu	alaṭṣu	'complaint'
eredi	erdi	'half'
eskila	iskla	'bell'
orotis	orots	'valient'
sorige . . .	sorgin	'soothsayer'

An old, perhaps somewhat sporadic change of [l] and [r] between vowels evidenced in loan words occurred in Basque:

Latin	Basque
angelus	aingeru
caelum	seru
colus	goru
pala	bara
voluntatem	borondate[14]

Some Iberian words formally similar to Basque and perhaps common to both languages may display the original [l]:

Iberian	Basque	
akel (akeli-adin)	aker̦	'billy-goat'
alaun	arau	'this,' 'circumstances'
balan	baran	'courageous' ?
elara-	erara	'in the manner of'
		era 'manner' - -ara.

Basque [belts] from an earlier *[beles]? (Aquitanian [beles]) suggests syncope occurred before [l] > [r]/v_v, thus preventing the change.

In some Basque dialects the sequence [rts] occurs as in *bertse* 'another, other' but is reduced to [st] in western dialects where the word is *beste*.[15] The change of [rts] to [st] seems to have taken place via *[rst], i.e., by metathesis followed by the loss of [r]. The intermediate stage of [rst] seems to have occurred in Iberian. Compare:

Basque	[borts]	'five'
W. Basque	[bost]	
Iberian	[borste]	
Aquitanian	[borsei]	

In some seemingly ancient Basque compounds [-n] of the first member disappears before a consonant or becomes [r] before a vowel, compare:

agin	'tooth'	agika	'denticulated'
belaun	'knee'	belaurikatu	'kneeled'
egun	'day'	egubakots	'Friday'
iaun	'señor'	iauregi	'palace'16

The loss or substitution of [-n] as the second member of a compound may also have occurred in Iberian, although, as in Basque, exceptions seem to have existed, leading to such variations as;

ildu-beles	*ildun-beles
ildu-tas	*ildun-tas
ildur-adin	*ildun-adin

but note also *illur-tibas* presumably from **ildun-tibas* on the Ascoli Bronze.

An Iberian-Latin name from Catalonia, *M. Iunius Iaurbeles,*17 may have a connection with Basque [iaun] but where [-r] instead of [-n] or [ø] indicates fluctuation. The first letter in the name *Iaur* on the inscription, however, is problematic. Note, also, that in other names on the Ascoli bronze such as *Adin-gibas* no change occurred. If during this period a modification was in progress, however, it must have followed the ordering [-n] > [-r] > [ø]. Compare also other Iberian sequences that seem to conform to the pattern, *ildu-koite, ildur-o,* and *ildu-ni* and some that do not, e.g., *ildun-bar.*

Iberian and Basque phonological similarities may translate into at least one correspondence that obtains between words in both languages. In environments where Iberian has [s] or [ş], Basque has [s], [ş] or [ts]. [tş].

Iberian   **Basque**

abaş	apats	'vase'
alatesu	alatsu	'complaint' also cf. *alatu* 'curse'18 and *ala* 'complaint'
arse	arts	'bear'
aş- (aşgandis)	atş	'breath'

123

ausa	autş	'ashes'
baiteşir	baitetşi	'grant, sanction, approve'
balşti-	baltşa	'mud, mire, mess'
bel/beles	belts	'black, dark'
berşa	bertse	'other'
bioş	biots	'heart'
borste	borts	'five'
gasi	gatsi	'salt'
ilş	iltse	'to die'
iş- (işbinai)	its	'word'
garse	gartsa	'heron'
kirşto	kirtsi, kirtsi-katu	'irritate, provoke'
-kuşu (kutitukuşu)	kutşu	'contagion' cf. *kusu* 'relative' *kuts* 'silent'
gurş	gurts	'culto'
okaş (okaştiker)	okats	'billy goat'
sikenştis	sikintsu	'impure, foul'
sorse-	sortsi	'eight'
urs- (ursteku)	urtsi	'god, thundergod'
unsir	untsi	'boat' cf. *untsiratu* "to embark'
us-	utsi	'allow'
uşta (uştalari)	utşta	'only'

Some interesting parallels between Basque and Iberian also occur on the morphological level. Among Iberian coin inscriptions is the suffix -*tar* or -*dar*, as in *Iltirtar* a form not unlike Basque -*tar* in the word *Bilbotar* 'a native of Bilbao.' The Iberian sequences *anusa aren* seem to find a parallel in the Basque -*aren* the definite genitive singular morpheme.

Basque morphological processes utilized the feature of infixation, compare;

suen	'he used to have it'
suten	'third line up from bottom'
du	'he has it'
ditu	'he has them'

Infixation may have been a viable process in Iberian

> banir
> bantir

and was perhaps sometimes coupled with metathesis if the resulting form was contrary to rules of phonology:

gani	gadin	ni > in/d- ?
gari	gadir	ri > ir/d- ?
gasi	gadis	si > is/d- ?

thus avoiding sequences of *dn, dr, ds*? Hence *baise > *baidse > baides*? Lack of meaning for Iberian words, however, renders morphophonemic statements of any kind to the realm of something somewhat less than a hypothesis.

Basque verbal forms sometimes utilize the infix *-ra-* with a kind of weak causative value in the sense of allowing something to happen:

ikusi	'to see'	i-ra-kutsi	'allow to see'
ekari	'to carry'	e-ra-kari	'allow to carry'

There is a hint of a similar type of infixation in Iberian:

ckar	o-ra-kar	
ses-	s-ar-es-	(saresu)
eber-	eb-ar-er	
kate-	ka-ra-te	
asun-	as-ar-un-	(asarunki)
osati	os-ar-ti-	(osartinyi)
ete	et-ar-e[19]	

Iberian words containing a form of the sequence *bait* seem to parallel the phonological rules of Basque *bait* and, in both languages, respond to certain constraints which inhibit the occurrence of certain consonant clusters, compare Iberian

bai-	*bait-*
baila	baite
baikar	baites
bainybar	baiti-
bais	baiturane
baise-	baitolo

There seems little advantage in attempting to compare the forms in the two languages on a semantic level since such a relationship is not demonstrable, but the following formal similarities inferred for Iberian suggest a certain congruency.

In Basque the prefix *bait-* obeys certain phonological rules:

bait > bai / ___ +consonant
biat - du   > baitu
bait - gare   > baikare
bait - nago   > bainago
bait - litake   > bailitake

that is, *-t* > *-ø/*___+consonant.

The rule avoids consonant clusters alien to Basque such as [td], [tg], [tn], [tl], etc. Note, however, that [ts] occurs in Basque and the rule does not apply when the following sound is [s].

bait - siren > baitsiren

Iberian sequences containing *bait-* seem to behave in a manner similar to Basque. The word *durane* occurs a number of times in Iberian documents and we also find *baiturane* which might be surmised is the result of *bait + durane > baiturane.* The sequence *-gar/-kar* occurs in Iberian as does the word *baikar* and may be the result of *bait + gar > baikar.*

Comparing such words as *ybariaikis* and *teybarese* we seem to be able to isolate a morpheme or morphemes *ybar.* The word *bainybar* then appears to consist of *bai-n-ybar* suggesting *bait + n-ybar > bainybar.* Also attested in Iberian the word *baila,* may stem from *bait + la > baila..*20

Basque [gaits] 'evil, harmful' appearing as the first member of a compound before a consonant, becomes [gais]. This word may be compared with Iberian in both form and distribution.

Iberian	Basque	
gais-kar	gais-gari	'harmful
gaiṣ-kata	gais-kata	'wound'
gais-egin	gaits-egin	'do evil'
gaiṣ-esa	gaits-etṣa	'misanthropist'

126

In this case, as in others however, even when Iberian words seem obviously somehow related to Basque there still remains the major difficulty in extracting meaning from the Iberian form. The polysemous nature of words coupled with semantic change obfuscates a clear and concise interpretation of the Iberian lexicon. A sequence of letters on the Lead Tablet from Liria reads:

gaisurargetan : sakariskar

This inscriptional sequence seems to contain a string of Basque related morphemes such as [gais], [ur], [argi] and perhaps the suffix [-etan] yet the sequence on the whole is not Basque and presents no clear semantic interpretation in Iberian. Is the form *gaisur* one word relating to Basque [gaitsuru] 'a unit of measurement' and perhaps a borrowed word, or is it [gaits + ur] ([ur] 'water'), and so on.

Another example of a near fit between Iberian and Basque is the word *geitesnaura* (both languages show the alternation [gait/geit]) where Basque [esnaur] seems to correspond to Iberian -*esnaur*-. The Basque word signifying 'ruminate' (related to [esna] 'milk') seems a rather unlikely candidate, however, because of its meaning. A more plausible word in Basque would be [gaitserauntsi] ([gaits-eraun-tsi] 'slander or injure a person's reputation' or [gaitseran] ([gaits-eran]) 'speak evil.'

The seemingly more plausible explanation also requires more dissimilarities between the words:

Iberian　　geitesnaru-

Basque　　gaitseraun

suggesting processes of metathesis, i.e., [se] ~ [es] and [raun] ~ [naur].[21]

The Iberian forms *gai, gaio* and *geitiatelu* might find an echo in Basque [gai] 'material, subject, means,' [gaio] 'wooden club' (among other meanings), [gailu] 'suitable, worthy' (compare also Basque [iate] 'eat'), [geio] 'more,' [kai] 'destined for,' etc. The word *gaibigait* where *bi* = [bi] 'two,' is clearly reminiscent of Basque.

While Iberian and Basque lexical and phonological features demonstrate certain characteristics in common, other aspects of the languages, in a comparative framework, lack congruency. Among the most obvious distinguishing morphological aspects of Basque such as the nominal case system, pronouns, the tense system or the analytic and periphrastic features of the verbs, there is little to compare with Iberian.[22] If Iberian had a case system it is unknown; no pronouns have been identified; tense and tense markers remain undiscovered, and verb morphology is still a mystery. Even the grammatical categories of noun, adjective, verb, preposition, and so on, constitute an unknown quantity.

While Basque is essentially a subject-object-verb language

> Neskak ogia ian   du
> the girl the   bread eaten has

nothing concrete can be said about Iberian syntax. Word relationships remain at present in a nether-world whose resurrection, with current knowledge, seems improbable.[23]

Nor can anything verifiable be said of Iberian stress, tone, intonation, etc.. Nothing of these linguistic features was recorded among the Iberian texts thus leaving no opportunity for comparison.[24]

FOOTNOTES

[1]See Chapter 1.

[2]Substratum hypotheses have been taken to great lengths in efforts to explain similarities between Iberian, Basque, Berber and other various lexical forms (place names, personal names) found throughout the Mediterranean basin. For example, a Euro-African substratum was envisaged to explain such similarities between Spain, France, Italy and North Africa and dating back to about 10,000 B.C. Euro-African speakers were 'covered over' around the third millennium B.C. by Hispano-Caucasian peoples migrating from the east, and relationships between Basque and Iberian and Caucasian languages can still be seen from this. For details, see Hubschmid 1960 and 1960a and various other of his papers.

[3]The point of view entertained by Bosch Gimpera 1957 considered the Iberian language and people to have been of African origin and the Basques of Pyrenean extraction.

[4]Note also the presence of [h] in Basque dialects north of the Pyrenees.

[5]See Michelena 1977 pp. 371 ff.

6This phonological similarity was first pointed out by Schuchardt as early as 1899. See Michelena *op. cit.,* p. 281-2.

7Aquitanian *Hannac* is problematic since the word appears to be incomplete.

8Borrowed words of more recent vintage may retain alien sequences. See Michelena *op .cit.,* p. 347 ff.

9See Untermann 1975 Vol. II pp. 46ff, for treatment of loan words in Iberian. The syllabic nature of Iberian occlusive signs required an orthographic vowel between sequences such as *b-r.*

10For this word on an inscription from Azaila, see Gómez-Moreno *Misceláneas* 1949 p. 295.

11See Michelena *op. cit.,* p. 347.

12*op. cit.,* p. 357-8.

13For this word, see Gómez-Moreno *op. cit.,* no. 31. Some phonetic distinction may have been maintained between [1] from [ld] and the original [l]. The incompleteness of the change in Basque is evident in words that still contain the sequence, e.g., *aldi* 'time.' See Michelena *op. cit.,* p. 359.

14*op. cit.* p. 312 for these and other words and their usage in various dialects.

15Maluquer, after Vives, records the Iberian word *bersa.* No. 360.

16Michelena, *op. cit.,* p. 309.

17*Op. cit.,* p. 547.

18Posited as a Basque form by Fletcher Valls 1980.

19Iberian forms in the right hand column could be names or common nouns derived from verbs. Variations of *ar* and *ra* seem to adhere to the rule *ra* > *ar*/con___, i.e., *ra* after a vowel and *ar* after a consonant. What appear to be stems or roots in the left-hand column occur in *sesa, şesdir-, eberka, katetasko, asuneyie, etedur.* Note also *etesilir* and *et-ar-is.*

20For the formation of *bait-* in Basque, see Lafitte p. 405.
    Note the sequence of morphemes *tur*/*bailura* on the Alcoy Lead

Tablet. Does *bait* > *bai* before *l?* Perhaps Iberian *baise* < *bait-se,* etc., cf. *baiseldun* where the same kind of phonological rule applicable to Basque *e + i* > *e* seems to occur here **biat-se-ildun.* Cf. also **urke-isker* > *urkesker.*
Note also that Basque *baila* 'official, magistrate' comparable to Iberian *baila,* has been perceived as related to Latin *baiulus.*

[21]Basque [gaiskin] 'bad' and Iberian *kaişaki* listed by Fletcher Valls 1981 p. 124 display close formal similarities. Cf. also Basque[gaistu] 'to become evil' [[gaistagin] 'wrong-doer' and [gaitsarasi] 'to make angry.'

[22]For a somewhat less than convincing morpho-syntactic comparison of Iberian and Basque, see Pattison.

[23]Even when Iberian and Basque seem to agree on a lexical level, simple syntactic relationships may remain unclear:

Iberian	geietisia	
Basque	isigaits	'brave'

[24]For aspects of suprasegmental features in Basque, see Michelena 1977 and Jacobsen.

Chapter 9

THE DEMISE OF THE ANCIENT HISPANIC LANGUAGES

The subjugation of the Iberian peninsula by foreign interests began in historical times with the extension into the interior of Carthaginian control from their foothold at Cádiz. Under Hamilcar Barca, the southwest was secured, and upon his death in about 228 B.C., his son-in-law, Hasdrubal, continued if in a less bellicose manner the expansionist policy, and founded a new port at Mastia. With the assassination of Hasdrubal, Carthaginian power fell into the hands of Hannibal who persisted in the suppression of the Hispanic tribes, finding the central and northern Celts and the Basques more intractable than the Mediterranean coastal peoples. His defeat on the plains of Zama in 202 B.C. by a Roman army under the command of Scipio, brought to an end the Second Punic War and, with Carthage exhausted, the Romans gained unrestricted access to the western Mediterranean and the Hispanic peninsula.

When the Romans arrived in Spain, Celtiberian expansion and its concomitant domination of neighboring autocthonous peoples was under way. For some tribes, the Romans were viewed as liberators, for others, oppressors. To these conditions the Roman axiom of 'divide and conquer' was well suited. Hispanic tribes fought alongside the legions as well as against them, and many did both in different times and circumstances.

The Roman conquest took place in three general phases: by around 200 B.C. Rome dominated the Iberian Mediterranean littoral from the Pyrenees to western Baetica. In a second assault, the meseta was subdued, ending with the fall of the Celtiberian town of Numantia in 133 B.C. The final conquest terminated around 25 A.D. and resulted in the subjugation of the Cantabrian region. Over this protracted period of time, various generations of the indigenous Hispanic population gradually abandoned their traditions and adopted the Roman way of life. However, in regions of difficult access such as the interior villages of the Pyrenees and Cantabrian mountains, native traditions continued longer and Roman penetrations into the Basque territories were relatively superficial and offered little particular inducement to the populations to modify their cultural characteristics.

In Galicia, preRoman villages and life-styles continued into the period of the late Empire of the fourth and fifth centuries. Complete Romanization was also late in coming to the Balearic Islands where the old Talaiotic cultures flourished well into the Christian millennium.

In other regions of the peninsula, especially the Mediterranean coastal areas, the indigenous peoples moved into the prosperous Roman towns, abandoning their hilltop villages in favor of more easy living. The transformation was relentless and the local cultures and languages gradually disappeared.

The Roman way was so thoroughly adopted in Spain and the fusion of the races so complete that before long, Romans born in Spain would rule over the Empire and the conquest of the Latin language, at least in its popular form as spoken by soldiers, merchants, farmers and bureaucrats, was as successful as the ultimate triumph of the Roman legions.

If the indigenous languages of Spain and Portugal survived much after the time of Augustus, there is no record of them with the exception of Basque and a few northern Celtic enclaves. Written Iberian seems to have disappeared by the first few decades of the first century A.D. or before, and from this time on, the Latin alphabet and Roman inscriptions dominated completely.

The linguistic legacy of the ancient Iberians in the later developments of the Neo Latin peninsular languages seems, at best, obscure and unportentous. The reduction of the consonant cluster [mb] > [m], for example, the emerging Romance languages of Spain (cf. Latin *inter ambus* > Aragonese *intramos; lumbu* > Catalan *llom,* etc.) could have been brought about by bilingual Iberians whose own speech appears to have undergone this change. The origin of such changes are often debatable, however, and the above can be taken as only a possible explanation among others.

In the realm of onomastics and especially place names, Iberian influence is more concrete. While most place names inscribed, for example on Iberian coins, have since disappeared through loss or replacement, a few have persisted to the present day, cf.

Iberian	Latin	Modern Spanish
baitolo	Baetulo	Badalona
barkeno	Barcino	Barcelona
iltirta	Ilerda	Lérida[1]

The influence of the Celtic language on emergent peninsular Romance has been studied and written about to a far greater degree than Iberian owing to the fact that the language is known and the information more accessible. Sometimes attributed to bilingual Celtic Hispano-Latin speakers were the sonorization of Latin intervocalic voiceless occlusives, the weakening of voiced occlusives, and the reduction of geminates, cf.

$$pp > p > b > \text{b̶}$$

$$tt > t > d > \text{d̶}$$

$$kk > k > g > \text{g̶}$$

A similar process generally referred to as lenition occurred in Old Celtic among consonants in intervocalic position, in word initial position when the preceding word ended in a vowel, and other specific phonological environments. The various Celtic languages demonstrate this fact. Compare Welsh:

Old Celtic	Welsh
p	b
t	d, Θ
k	g, X
b	b̶
d	d̶
g	ø2

Early examples of lenition in Romance words in Celtic areas, documented between the second and the tenth centuries, point to circumstantial evidence of an affinity between the processes in both languages, cf. *imudavit < inmutavit, perpeduo < perpetuo, lebra < lepra ,eglesia < ecclesia, sebaratus < separatus.* Most of the examples of this kind come from the north and central regions of the peninsula.[3]

The process of lenition became widespread in the western Romance languages, cf. Spanish *vida < vita, sabe < sapit, vaca < vacca.* It has been suggested that the retention of Latin voiceless occlusives in Aragonese and Bearnese was due to the aspirated nature of voiceless occlusives in ancient Iberian, a feature transferred to Hispano-Latin by bilingual speakers and thus inhibiting sonorization.

There is of course no way of knowing if Iberian voiceless occlusives were aspirated or not. The ancient inscriptions reveal no such information and only risky inferences can be drawn from Basque which show points in contact with Iberian, and which was thought to have had aspirated voiceless occlusives still evident in some dialects. Direct Basque influence is considered by some to have been the cause of the retention of the voiceless occlusives in this region along with the late continued use of the voiceless intervocalic consonants in Castille and Rioja.4

A number of diverse phonological modifications have been imputed to Celtic substratum influence, especially those revolving around palatalization processes. The palatalization of /-ll-/ and /l-/ to /λ/, as in Castillian *bella* /béλa/ from Latin *bella;* and *lluna* from *luna* in Catalan, areas of Aragón, Asturias, Leon and Galicia; the reduction of /pl-/ and /kl-/ to /λ/; the palatalization of /-nn-/ to /ñ/, and so on, are phenomena initially associated with Celtic areas of the peninsula. Similar changes can be found among the various Celtic languages as well as the loss of /-n-/ and /-l-/ which was also associated with Galician and Portuguese.

The vocalization of the Latin consonant cluster /-kt-/ in Gaul and in the Hispanic peninsula *nocte* /nokte/, resulting in French *nuit,* Spanish *noche* (where /kt/ > /yt/ > /č/), and Portuguese *noite*) have also been sometimes relegated to Celtic influence. The Celtic languages seem to have undergone a similar change, cf. Latin *lacte* (French *lait,* Spanish *leche,* Portuguese *leite*), and Welsh *llaeth*, and Irish *lacht.*5

The degree of influence Hispano-Celtic had on the emerging peninsular Romance languages remains a subject of contention. It is only in the domain of Hispano-Romance vocabulary that clear and direct Celtic influence may be unequivocally identified. While most of the Celtic words that have persisted in Spain and Portugal entered Popular Latin from Gaul and were then diffused throughout the Empire, some nevertheless were due to the Celtic substratum in Spain. Most of the surviving Celticisms refer to place names, cf. Deva, a river in Guipúzcoa corresponding to Latin *divus* from **deivos;* Arganza, a sometime river in Asturias; Celtigos, a toponymic recorded several times in the province of Coruña, and once in the province of Lugo; Betanzos from Brigantium, Nenebrega from Mundobriga, and a number of others. The Portuguese-Galician word *tona* 'rind,' appears to have a cognate in Welsh *ton* and Irish *tonn.*6

Apart from the Basque region, the thorough Romanization of the Iberian peninsula is evident in the dearth of substratum influence from the preRoman languages. Perhaps because of the early Romanization of Spain and Portugal, allowing centuries of cultural and linguistic reinforcement from Rome, coupled with the tenacious and ubiquitous hold of the Church on the inhabitants in whose schools, seminaries and sermons Latin thrived, substratum influences that other circumstances might have fostered were not successful.

It is no doubt at least partially true that the Latin speech patterns of local areas differed from one another to some unknown extent, due to local substratum influences, and that these differences contributed to the mosaic of languages and dialects found today on the peninsula. To pinpoint these differences of today in the poorly understood languages of antiquity, however, is a formidable task.

In many cases, the evidence for substratum influence has been at best inconclusive, either because the particular modification in question can be explained without benefit of a substratum influence, or because the substratum language seemingly responsible for a certain modification is not well known at the relevant chronological period.

For example, to maintain that the Celtic languages were responsible for nasalization in Portuguese and certain areas of Galicia, without evidence that the Celts in these areas nasalized vowels, seems to beg the question. Influences from Basque on the vocabulary and phonology of Hispano-Romance can be more adequately demonstrated, but here also problems arise.

Basque place names have given way before Roman names from the earliest period. The name Zaragoza, for example, was derived from Latin Caesar Augusta, replacing the older name Salduba. In some cases, both Romance and Basque place names coexisted: Pamplona 'Pompeii's town,' is known to Basque speakers as Iruña 'the good town.'

A number of words occur in peninsular languages whose origins are not accounted for, cf. *manteca, abarca, cama* and *brujo.* They may, of course, derive from Iberian, but this tentative conclusion can only be reached by process of elimination.

While some Hispano-Romance words seem to be derived from Basque, it is not always clear whether they may have been incorporated into Hispano-Romance from Iberian and subsequently borrowed by Basque. Besides place names and personal names such as Iñigo and Javier, a few lexical items considered to have been of Basque origin but with the above-stated consideration in mind are:

Spanish	Basque	Spanish	Basque
nava	naba	arroyo	erreka
vega[7]	ibaiko	zorro	azeri
cachorro	txakur	izquierda	ezker
zamarra	zamar	bizarro	bizar[8]
pizarra	lapitz-arri[9]	laya	lai(a)

Many of the modifications in Castilian Spanish appear to have been innovations which gave this dialect its unique characteristics *vis-à-vis* other Hispano-Romance idioms. The circumstances in which these changes took place seem to point directly to Basque influence when it is kept in mind that the north of Old Castile, birthplace of Castilian, was a small isolated region up to and throughout the Middle Ages, whose inhabitants were largely bilingual Basque-Romance speakers. Of interest also is the fact that in the dialects of Gascon which occupy the ancient territory of Aquitania, many of the same kinds of changes occurred.

Written documentation in the Basque language dates back to the sixteenth century with a few glosses from the tenth century.10 Back to that time it seems to have had a system of voiceless sibilants differing from Castilian of the period in its lack of voiced sibilants. Basque speakers (according to the substratum view) produced the Castilian voiced sounds as voiceless in conformity with their own language.

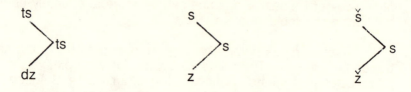

These mergers substantially altered the medieval consonantal paradigm of Castilian.

The absence of voiced sibilants in High Aragonese can also be attributed to Basque but in other regions where mergers occurred, as in Asturo-Leonese, these must then be imputed to later Castilian influence.

Basque did not contain initial /r-/ and borrowed words display a prothetic vowel in these circumstances e.g., *arrazoi* from Spanish *razón.* Old Spanish documents from the north and central regions contain words, mostly proper names, which appear to utilize a prothetic vowel before /r/, e.g., *Aramirus* 'Ramiro,' *Arremon* 'Ramón.' The prothetic vowel is also characteristic of High Aragonese, cf. [arriɣe] 'reir,' arriɣacuelo] 'raichuelo.' Similarly, Gascon substituted /arr-/ for Latin /r-/.

One of the difficulties with the substratum approach as an explanation of modifications in Castilian Spanish is that some changes of the same kind also occurred in other dialects which were not subject to Basque influence. Nevertheless, it has been argued that Castilian, enhanced by its status as the prestige dialect, was responsible for these changes elsewhere. Such modifications that began in Old Castile, spread southward, such as the change from /f/ to /h/, the merger of /b/ and /v/ (both sometimes attributed to Basque influence) and the devoicing of sibilants.11

A surprising characteristic of Basque on the Spanish side of the Pyrenees is the close resemblance it shows to Modern Castilian in both the nature and distribution of sound patterns. Among the vowels both languages display a simple five-vowel system /a/, /e/, /i/, /o/, and /u/, while among the consonants both contain similar labial and dental sounds, palatalized /ñ/ and / λ /, single and multiple (or trilled) /r/ sounds, and neither have voiced fricatives. Compare Basque and Modern Castilian, where the sound units corresponding to the latter are placed in parentheses: (Basque /f/ is found in recent borrowed words.)

p (p)	t (t)	ts	tṣ	tš (tš)		k (k)
b (b)	d (d)					g (g)
f (f)	(Ɵ)	s (s)	ṣ	š		(X)
m (m)	n (n)			ñ (ñ)		
	l (l)			λ (λ)		
	r (r)					
	rr (rr)					

Note that Castilian /Ɵ/ and /X/ are recent reflexes of Medieval Spanish /ts/ and /š/ respectively, indicating divergence from an earlier even closer system of parallel sounds.

From a distributional point of view, the two languages also have features in common. The place of articulation of nasals is neutralized before consonants leading to homorganic clusters, the opposition between /l/ and /λ/ is neutralized before and after consonants and in final position. The opposition of /r/ and /rr/ is effective only in intervocalic position and neutralized elsewhere. Basque does not support /s/ plus an occlusive initial consonant (except in borrowed words, e.g., *skiatu* 'to ski') a condition that coincides with the development of prothetic vowels in the Romance languages. Groups of consonants in word initial position also fairly well coincide with Spanish in the distribution of occlusive plus /r/ or /l/.

The evolution of the Castilian dialect of Spanish, whose history has been intimately linked with Basque speakers, appears to have been in part molded by this contact. Ancient Iberian and Basque, especially in the regions of the Pyrenean Mountains, and perhaps well before the advent of writing on the peninsula, also seem to have been in intimate enough contact, perhaps through bilingual Iberian/Basque speakers, to produce some linguistic blending.

137

FOOTNOTES

[1]For these and other examples, see Untermann 1975 Vol. I.

[2]Lewis and Pedersen pp. 127 ff.

[3]For these and further examples, see Tovar 1961, p. 80; Menéndez-Pidal 1950, pp. 45-7; Schmoll 1959, p. 91; Lejeune 1955, p. 132, among others. Martinet presents arguments *pro* and *con* concerning Celtic substratum influences in Spain. See also Baldinger, pp. 193-204.

[4]Another view maintains that sonorization occurred in Aragonese but later devoicing took place.

[5]For Celtic substratum influences and relevant bibliography, see and Jungemann.

Gallego-Portuguese shows the loss of intervocalic [-n-] and [-l-] and the palatalization of [pl], [fl] to [č] > [š]. This change occurred only in the northwest corner of the peninsula. The loss of [-n-] and [-l-] can be documented as far back as the ninth and tenth centuries respectively. (The loss of [-n-] occurred also in Gascon.)

In the northwest the names of deities were preserved into the Roman epoch (see Untermann 1980b and Albertos). The preservation of certain linguistic items in this part of the peninsula were no doubt due to the late and 'weak' Romanization of the area. Even today, certain pagan rites continue to exist in this part of Spain and Portugal in the form of games, see Baldinger p. 150.

[6]Entwistle, p. 40.

[7]Old Spanish *vaica, vaiga.*

[8]*bizarro* 'gallant,' *bizar* 'beard.'

[9]*lapitz* [lapits] from Latin *lapideus* and Basque *arri* 'stone.'

[10]San Millán de la Cogolla provided the first vernacular documents in Spanish, *Glosas Emilianenses* in the tenth century. Some words had Basque glosses.

[11]The lack of [v] in Basque is indicated by Latin loan words: *vagina > magina, ventura > mentura, vindicare > mendekatu.*

BIBLIOGRAPHICAL REFERENCES CITED

Albertos Firmat, Ma. "Organizaciones suprafamiliares en la Hispania antigua." *Studia Archaeológica.* Universidad de Valladolid (1979).
_____. "La onomástica de la celtibéria." *Actas del II coloquio sobre lenguas y culturas prerromanas de la península ibérica.* Acta Salamanticensia. Filosofía y Letras. 113. Salamanca (1979).

Allières, J. *Les Basques.* 2d ed. Presses Universitares de France (1977).

Arribas, A. *The Iberians.* London: Thames and Hudson (1964).

Baldinger, K. *La formación de los domínios lingüísticos en la península ibérica.* Madrid: Gredos (1963).

Beltrán Lloris, M. "Problems en torno al signo ibérico Y" *Miscelanea Arqueológica.* Vol. I Barcelona (1974).

Beltrán Martínez, A. "El alfabeto monetal llamado 'libio-fenice'." *Numisma* 4, 13 (1954) pp. 49-63.

Beltrán Villagrasa, P. "Sobre un interesante vaso escrito de San Miguel de Liria." *Servicio de Investigación Prehistórica* Num. 8. Valencia (1942).

Bosch-Gimpera, P. *El poblamiento antiguo y la formacíon de los pueblos de españa.* Mexico: Imprenta Universitaria (1944).
_____. "Ibères, Basques, Celts." *Orbis* VI (1957), pp. 126-34.

Bouda, K. *Baskisch-Kaukasische Etymologien.* Heidelberg (1949).

Buck, C.D. *A Dictionary of Selected Synonyms in the Principal Indo-European Languages.* University of Chicago Press (1949).

Cabré Aguiló, J. <u>*Corpus Vasorum Hispanorum.*</u> Madrid (1944).

Caro Baroja, J. *Sobre la historia del desciframiento de las escrituras hispánicas.* Madrid: Actas y Memorias de la Sociedad Español Etnografía y Prehistoria, Vol. 21 (1946).

Charpentier, L. *Le Mystère Basque.* Paris: Robert Laffont (1975).

Corominas, J. *Diccionario crítico etimológico de la lengua castellana.* Berne: Francke (1954).

Cuadrado, E. "Origin y desarrollo de la cerámica de barniz rojo en el mundo tartésico." *Tartessos.X simposium internacional de prehistoria peninsular.* Barcelona (1969).

Enciclopédia linguística hispánica (ELH) Vol. I. Madrid: Consejo Superior de Investigaciones Científicas (1960).

Entwistle, W.J. *The Spanish Language.* London: Faber & Faber (1952).

Evans, D.E. "On the Celticity of some Hispanic personal names." *Actas del II coloquio sobre lenguas y culturas prerromanas de la península ibérica.* Acta Salmanticensia. Filosofía y Letras. 113. Salamanca (1979).

Gaulish Personal Names. Oxford (1967).

Faust, M. "Die Kelten auf der Iberischen Halbinsel: Sprachliche Zeugnisse." *Madrider Mitteilungen* (1975).

_____. "Cuestiones generales de toponimia prerromana. *Actas del I coloquio sobre lenguas y culturas prerromanas de la península ibérica.* Acta Salmanticensia. Filosofía y Letras. 95. Salamanca (1976).

Fletcher Valls, D. *Inscripciones ibéricas de Museo de Prehistoria de Valencia.* Estudios Ibéricos No. 2. Valencia (1953). 2d ed. (1985).

_____. Cinco inscripciones ibéricas de Los Villares. Valencia: Archivo de Prehistórica Levantina XV (1978).

_____. *De nuevo sobre el signo ibérico Y.* Valencia: Depto. de Historia Antigua, Serie Arqueológica No. 6. Varia I (1979).

_____. *Los plomos ibéricos de Yátova.* Valencia: Servicio de Investigación Prehistórica, Diputación Provincial de Valencia Trabajos Varcos Num. 66 (1980).

_____. *Materiales de la necróplis Ibérica de Orleyl.* Valencia: Servicio de Investigación Prehistórica, Diputación Provincial de Valencia, Trabajos varios. Num. 70 (1981).

_____. *El plomo Ibérico de Mogente.* Valencia: Servico de Investigación Prehistórica, Diputación Provincial de Valencia. Trabajos varios. Num. 76 (1982).

Fleuriot, L. "La grande inscription celtibère de Botorrita." *Actas del II coloquio sobre lenguas y culturas prerromanas de la península ibérica.* Acta Salmanticensia. Filosofía y Letras. 113. Salamanca (1979).

García y Bellido, A. *Arte ibérico en España.* Madrid: Espasa-Calpe (1980).

Gómez-Moreno, M. *Misceláneas: historia, arte, arqueología.* Madrid (1949).

_____. *La escritura Bastulo-Turdetana.* Madrid: Ediciones de Archivos, Bibliotecas y Museos (1962).

Gorrochategui Churruca, J. *Estudie sobre la onómastica indígena de Aquitania.* Bilbao: Universidad de País Vasco (1984).

Houwink Ten Cate, Ph. H.J. *The Luwian Population Groups of Lydia and Cilicia Aspera during the Hellenistic Period.* Leiden: Brill (1965).

Hoz, J. "La epigrafía prelatina meridional en hispania." *Actas del I coloquio sobre lenguas y culturas prerromanas de la península ibérica.* Acta Salmanticensia. Filosofia y Letras. 95. Salamanca (1976).

_____. "Un hipótesis de trabajo sobre la escritura del Algarve." *Revista de la Universidad Complutense.* Vol. XXVI, No. 109 (1977).

_____. *Escritura e influencia clásica en los pueblos*

prerromanos de la península. Archivo español de Arqueología. Madrid (1979).

Hübner, E. *Monumenta Linguae Ibericae.* Berlin (1893).

Hubschmid, J. "Toponimia prerromana." *ELH* Vol. I (1960), pp. 447-99.

_____. *Mediterrane Substrate mit besonderer Berück sichtigung des Baskischen und der west-ostlichen Sprachbeziehungen.* Bern (1960a).

Jacobsen, W. "Rule Ordering in Vizcayan." Berkeley: University of California Linguistic Conference (1971).

Jannoray, J. *Ensérune: Etude des civilisations préromaines de la Gaule Méridional.* Paris (1955).

Jensen, H. *Sign Symbol and Script.* London: George Allen and Unwin Ltd. (1970).

Jungemann, F.H. *La teoría del sustrato y los dialectos hispano-romances y gascones.* Madrid: Gredos (1955).

Koch, M. Die Keltiberer und ihr historischer Kontext. *Actas del II coloquio sobre lenguas y culturas prerromanas de la península ibérica.* Acta Salmanticensia. Filosofía y Letras. 113. Salamanca (1979).

_____. *Tarschisch und Hispanien.* Berlin: Walter de Gruyter (1984).

Lafitte, P. *Grammaire Basque.* Bayonne: Ikas-Marengo Karrika Musée Basque (1979).

Lafon, R. "La lengua vasca." *ELH,* Vol. I (1960), pp. 67-100.

Lejeune, M. "Celtibérica." *Acta Salmanticensia Filosofía y Letras* VII, No. 4. Universidad de Salamanca (1955).

Lewis, H. and H. Pedersen. *A Concise Comparative Celtic Grammar.* Göttingen: Vandenhoeck & Ruprecht (1937).

Llobregat, E.A. "Los grafitos en escritura jónica e ibérica del este, del Museo de Alicante." *Revista de la Facultad de Filosofía y Letras de la Universidad de Valencia* XV (1965).

_____. *Contestania Ibérica* Instituto de Estudios Alicantinos, Series II, No. 2 (1972).

Maluquer de Motes, J. *Epigrafía prelatina de la península ibérica.* Instituto de Arqueología y Prehistoria. Universidad de Barcelona. Publicaciones eventuales. 12. (1968)

_____. *Tartessos.* Barcelona: Destino (1970).

Martinet, A. *Economie des Changements Phonétiques.* Berne: A. Francke (1955).

Menéndez-Pidal, R. *Orígenes del español.* Madrid: Espasa-Calpe (1950).

Michelena, L. *Fonética histórica vasca.* San Sebastian: Publicaciones del seminario Julio de Urquijo. Imprenta de la

Diputación de Guipúzcoa, 2d ed. (1977).

_____. *Sobre la historia de la lengua vasca.* San
Sebastian: Publicaciones del seminario Julio de Urquijo. Imprenta
de la Diputación de Guipúzcoa (1982).

Mukarovsky, H.G. "Baskisch and Berberisch." *Wiener Zeitschrift für
die Kunde des Morgenlandes (*1963-4) pp. 52-94.

Nicolini, G. *Les Ibères.* Librarie Arthème Fayard (1973).

Oliva Prat. "El nuevo plomo con inscripción ibérica hallado en
Ullastret." *Pyrene* 3 (1967).

Oroz Arizcuren, F.J. "Aurtxo Txikia Seaskan Dago" - Zum Basko-
Iberismus. *Romania Cantat,* Band II Interpretationen, pp. 555-82.

Pattison, W. "Iberian and Basque" Archivo de Prehistoria Levantina
Vol. XVI. Valencia (1981).

Pedersen, H. *The Discovery of Language.* Bloomington: Indiana
University Press (first published by Harvard University Press) (l93l).

Pulgram, E. *Italic, Latin, Italian 600 B.C. to A.D. 1260.*
Heidelberg: Carl Winter (1978).

Ramos Fernandez, R. "Inscripciones ibéricas de la Alcudia." *Archivo
de Prehistoria Levantina,* Vol. XII (1969), pp. 169-176.

Ruhlen, M. *A Guide to the Languages of the World.* Stanford
University: Language Universals Project (1975).

Schmoll, U. *Die Sprachen der Vorkeltischen Indogermanen
Hispaniens und das Keltiberische.* Wiesbaden: Otto
Harrassowitz (1959).

_____. *Die Südlusitanischen Inschriften.*
Wiesbaden: Otto Harrassowitz (1961).

Schuchardt, H. "Die Iberische Deklinations." *Sitzungsberichte der
philosopisch-historischen Klasse der Kaiserlichen Akademie der
Wissenschaften* CLVIT ii (1909) pp. 218-22.

Schwartz, S.P. *The PreLatin Dialect of Aquitania.* PhD.
dissertation, Cambridge, Mass.: Harvard University (1962).

Schwerteck, H. "Zur Deutung der Grossen Felsinschrift von Peñalba
de Villastar." *Actas del II coloquio sobre lenguas y culturas
prerromanas de la península ibérica.* Acta Salmanticensia.
Filosofía y Letra. 113. Salamanca (1979).

Sevilla, Rodriguez. "Posibles vestigios toponímicos de cultos célticos
en el norte de la península ibérica." *Memorias de Historia
Antigua III.* Universidad de Oviedo (1979).

Siles, J. "Sobre el signo ibéricoY " *Emérita* 49 (1981), pp. 75-96.

Solier, Y. "Découverte d'inscriptions sur plombs en écriture ibérique
dans un entrepôt de Pech Maho." *Revue Archéologique de
Narbonnaise* XII (1979).

Tovar, A. *The Ancient Languages of Spain and Portugal.* New
York: S.F. Vanni (1961).

Tuñón de Lara, M., M. Tarradell, and **J. Mangas.** *Historia de España: I. Introducción primeras culturas e hispania romana.* Barcelona: Labor (1980).

Untermann, J. *Monumenta Linguarum Hispanicarum.* Wiesbaden: Dr. Ludwig Reichert Verlag, Band I (1975), Band II (1980), Band III (to appear 1987?)

_____. "La Varietà Linguistica Nell'Iberia Preromana." *AIΩN.* Istituto Universitario Orientale. Napoli (1981).

_____. "La lengua ibérica." *Varia III* , Valencia (1984a).

_____. "Los celtiberos y sus vecinos occidentales." *Letras Asturianas* Vol. 13, Oviedo (1984b).

_____. *Navicula Tübingensis* (Studie in honorem Antonii Tovar). Tübingen: Gunter Narr Verlag (1984c), pp. 377-87.

_____. "Los teónimos de la región lusitano-gallega como fuente de las lenguas indígenas." *Actas del III Coloquio sobre Lenguas y Culturas Paleohispánicas.* Lisbon, 1980. Salamanca (1985a).

_____. "La gramática de los plomos ibéricos." *Actas del IV Coloquio sobre Lenguas y Culturas Paleohispánicas.* Vitoria (1985b).

Vallejo, J. "La escritura ibérica estado actual de su conocimiento." *Emérita* II (1943), pp. 461-75.

Verd, G.M., S.J. *Sobre la cuestión vascoibérica.* Seminario de Filología Vasca, Julio de Urquijo. Separata del Anuario XIV (1980), pp. 101-33.

Whatmough, J. *The Dialects of Ancient Gaul.* Harvard University Press (1970).

James Anderson has been Professor Linguistics at the University of Calgary for the past eighteen years. Much of his writing and research has focussed on Hispanic Languages, particularly those of ancient Spain and Portugal. Dr. Anderson has spent several years living in Spain and is very familiar with the languages and cultural history of that country.